THE LEARNING
RELATIONSHIP

To Lois,
With best wishes
+ good memories.

Biddy Youell

Tavistock Clinic Series

Margot Waddell (Series Editor)
Published and distributed by Karnac Books

Orders
Tel: +44 (0)20 7431 1075; Fax: +44 (0)20 7435 9076
Email: shop@karnacbooks.com
www.karnacbooks.com

THE LEARNING RELATIONSHIP

Psychoanalytic Thinking in Education

Biddy Youell

with contributions from the writings of
Hamish Canham

KARNAC

Chapter 1 reproduced from H. Canham, "'Where Do Babies Come From?' What Makes Children Want to Learn?", *Educational Therapy and Therapeutic Teaching*, Vol. 9 (2002), pp. 28–36, by permission of the Caspari Foundation.

Extracts in chapters 9 and 10 reproduced from H. Canham, "Group and Gang States of Mind", *Journal of Child Psychotherapy*, Vol. 28, No. 2 (2002), pp. 113–129, by permission of Routledge.

Chapter 12 reproduced from B. Youell, "Assessment, Evaluation and Inspection in School: A Psychodynamic. Perspective", *International Journal of Infant Observation*, Vol. 8, No. 1 (2005), pp. 59–68, by permission.

"Death of a Naturalist" (p. 12) reproduced from Seamus Heaney, *Death of a Naturalist* (London: Faber & Faber, 1966), by permision of Faber & Faber.

First published in 2006 by
Karnac Books
118 Finchley Road
London NW3 5HT

British Library Cataloguing in Publication Data

A C.I.P. for this book is available from the British Library

ISBN-13: 978-1-85575-227-6
ISBN-10: 1-85575-227-1

Edited, designed, and produced by Communication Crafts

Printed in Great Britain

www.karnacbooks.com

CONTENTS

v

SERIES EDITOR'S PREFACE

Since it was founded in 1920, the Tavistock Clinic has developed a wide range of developmental approaches to mental health which have been strongly influenced by the ideas of psychoanalysis. It has also adopted systemic family therapy as a theoretical model and a clinical approach to family problems. The Clinic is now the largest training institution in Britain for mental health, providing postgraduate and qualifying courses in social work, psychology, psychiatry, and child, adolescent, and adult psychotherapy, as well as in nursing and primary care. It trains about 1,700 students each year in over 60 courses.

The Clinic's philosophy aims at promoting therapeutic methods in mental health. Its work is based on the clinical expertise that is also the basis of its consultancy and research activities. The aim of this Series is to make available to the reading public the clinical, theoretical, and research work that is most influential at the Tavistock Clinic. The Series sets out new approaches in the understanding and treatment of psychological disturbance in children, adolescents, and adults, both as individuals and in families.

In significant ways, *The Learning Relationship* represents psychoanalytic thinking at its best. The work described draws on a

Tavistock-based course for teachers that has been running for over thirty years. Over those three decades a fertile two-way thoroughfare has developed.

Psychotherapist staff have immersed themselves in the problems, hazards, challenges, and satisfactions of the world of education, from primary to tertiary, from special needs to mainstream. The teachers themselves have been offered not only what most trainings lack—that is, a thorough understanding of the nature of children's psychological development and the characteristics of different ages and stages—but also insight into the troubled states of mind that affect most young people, whether expressed through difficulties in learning or in behaviour or both.

Teachers in particular will appreciate the immense wisdom and respect that underlies the authors' accounts of, for example, the emotional impact of change, separation, times of transition, bereavement, bullying, racial discrimination, and so forth. But parents, too, will derive insight and understanding from this account and from the fine balance achieved between the anxieties and pressures of contemporary educational settings and the potential fulfilment of being part of an institution in which containing relationships promote and sustain the "growing up" that children are doing both emotionally and cognitively.

This link between feelings and the capacity for thought lies at the heart of the book, whether in the individual or in the dynamics of the family, the staffroom, the group, or the institution as a whole. The chapters focus on the true meaning of education and its vital developmental role, in contrast to the target-driven pressures of curriculum delivery that can so often reduce these vital years to ones of stressful, test-orientated training. In so doing the book includes reflections not only on the psychoanalytic understanding of what makes children want to learn, but also on the nature of play and playfulness. It is this and the vividly observed examples of children and their happy and unhappy worlds that make these pages a learning experience in itself.

ACKNOWLEDGEMENTS

This book has been a long time in the writing, and I want to thank all those who have been tolerant of my slow progress and who have encouraged me to persevere. I am particularly grateful to the staff and students of the course on which this book is based—Emotional Factors in Learning and Teaching: Counselling Aspects in Education—and to everyone who has contributed observational material or a vignette from school life.

I want to thank Hamish Canham's widow, Hazel, for giving me his lecture notes and Dierdre Brown for deciphering his handwriting!

It is often suggested that everyone remembers one teacher as having a particular impact . . . for good or for ill. My history teacher at secondary school taught me to enjoy writing, and I am grateful to her for that. She was also one of the first to show me that it is possible to combine effective didactic teaching with genuine concern for the emotional experience of students.

My thanks are also due to Margot Waddell for her generosity as Series Editor, to Eric King of Communication Crafts, and to Karnac Books.

Introduction

This volume is a collection of papers, each of which is a version of a lecture previously given as part of the Tavistock course, "Emotional Factors in Learning and Teaching: Counselling Aspects in Education". The course, which is for teachers and others working in educational settings, has been running for more than thirty years. It began as a collaboration between Martha Harris, then Head of the Child Psychotherapy training at the Tavistock Clinic, and her husband, Roland Harris, an educationalist and writer. This partnership between clinical thinking and expertise in educational theory and practice continues to the present day, with child psychotherapists and educationalists working closely together.

The ideas underpinning the course were first elaborated by Isca Salzberger-Wittenberg, Gianna Henry, and Elsie Osborne in 1983 in *The Emotional Experience of Learning and Teaching*, a book that remains a valued, core text. This new volume, *The Learning Relationship*, represents an attempt to revisit some of the same themes and to set the applied psychoanalytic thinking in the current educational context. The idea for the book arose when Hamish Canham and I were joint organizing tutors of the course. Having recently qualified as child psychotherapists, Hamish and I shared an interest in making psychoanalytic ideas available to colleagues in non-clinical settings. His background was in residential social work, mine was in teaching. We had both been challenged by our experiences and, long before embarking on clinical training, had found considerable support in psychoanalytic understanding.

Our enthusiasm for the course and for this book arose from two sources. First, our clinical work with troubled and damaged children reminded us of the central importance of school experience in the lives of children and adolescents. In popular culture, psychoanalysis is often characterized as attributing every ill to adverse experiences in infancy. Although we would not want to understate the importance of early relationships in later development (see particularly chapters 1, 2, and 3), we had the idea for a book that would pay proper respect to the significance of formal education and would recognize the "therapeutic" potential of relationships between pupils and their teachers. Teachers are not—nor should they be—"therapists", but their relationships with the children they teach have enormous reparative as well as developmental potential.

The second motivating force was the recognition of just how challenging teaching is as a profession. The primary task sounds very simple when summed up as "delivering the curriculum", but the complexities are vast. As well as knowing their subject matter and being able to prepare interesting, engaging, age-appropriate lessons for mixed-ability groups, teachers have to cope with large numbers of children who are, by definition, in a process of constant change and development. There are significant numbers of children and young people who, to varying degrees, cannot learn or cannot conform to the norms of social behaviour. There is also the challenge of working with colleagues in groups and teams as part of complex institutions and the wider education service. There are innumerable dedicated, effective teachers, and yet, as a profession, teaching continues to attract negative projections. Individually, teachers are often appreciated; however, collectively, they are held responsible (like social workers) for many of society's ills.

Hamish and I, in our work together, shared a conviction that applied psychoanalytic thinking can make a major difference to teachers in helping them to bear the myriad projections to which they are subject. He and I planned the content of this book and divided the chapters in line with our particular interests and with the shape of the lecture series as taught on the course.

Sadly, we were not able to complete the project together as planned. Following Hamish Canham's tragic illness and death in 2003, I have continued to work on the book and am pleased to be able to include two chapters—chapters 1 and 4—that are entirely his work. (Chapter 4 is an edited version of a lecture he presented.) His influence on my thinking is evident in other parts of the text, and I want especially to acknowledge his work on groups and institutions, which I have referred to extensively in chapters 9 and 10.

Hamish's introductory chapter (chapter 1), which was first published in 2000 in *Educational Therapy and Therapeutic Teaching*, introduces a wide range of theories and themes that are explored further in later chapters. It is a full chapter, and readers who knew Hamish will recognize both his enthusiasm for literature and his rigorous psychoanalytic thinking. In chapter 2, I have sketched out a theoretical overview, introducing some key psychoanalytic concepts and the ways in which unconscious processes manifest themselves in the classroom.

Building on theories of learning in infancy, chapter 3 looks at the central importance of play to the young child and points to the links between play and learning in later development. In our discussions about the book, Hamish and I agreed that we would try to achieve a balance between, on the one hand, an emphasis on the inevitable anxiety and envy involved in learning and, on the other, full recognition of the "epistemophilic instinct" (Klein, 1931) and the pleasure of learning when it takes place in a containing relationship. In chapter 3, we see Timothy (the subject of an infant observation) in a phase of energetic, purposeful, and joyful development.

Chapters 4 and 5 focus on latency and adolescence, respectively. The developmental tasks are outlined, with particular reference to the dynamics that are likely to hold sway between child and parent, child and school, and teacher and learner. In this context, I allude to different kinds of learning and different states of mind that characterize these major developmental stages.

The relevance of beginnings, endings, and times of transition has been at the core of the course since its inception. Early separation from the primary carer is seen as a prototypical experience, and attention is drawn to the ways in which later loss and change re-evoke something of that first experience. Many students have commented that the thinking about beginnings and endings is among the most useful in terms of practical application. Not only does it inform their thinking about individual pupils who struggle with change, but it influences their wider planning and, sometimes, that of the whole institution (chapter 6).

Chapter 7 looks in more detail at the notion of the psycho-analytic "observational stance" and the usefulness of this kind of observation in the classroom. A lengthy illustration is included to show the way in which observations are discussed in "work-discussion" seminars. Chapter 8 explores some of the factors involved in teaching children with special educational needs and again makes use of material from work-discussion presentations.

The second half of the volume reflects the curriculum in the second year of the course at the Tavistock. The focus shifts to thinking about the impact on the individual of group and institutional dynamics (chapter 9). Chapter 10 offers a psychoanalytic perspective on projective processes in schools: on gangs, bullying, and racism. Chapter 11 examines the role of the family group and some of the factors that affect relationships between parents and schools.

The final two chapters reflect some of my personal preoccupations. Chapter 12 is a reprint of a paper first published in 2005 in the *International Journal of Infant Observation and its Applications*. The purpose of the paper is to elucidate the internal dynamics that are stirred up by being assessed or inspected. However, I am very aware that over the years I have become increasingly conscious of the external framework within which teachers are working. Politicians emphasize the importance of the role of the teacher but are quick to criticize. In fact, the current socio-political context is rife with contradictions. Teachers are presented not as the distant authoritarian figures of the past (backed up by a range of punishments, most of which are no longer legal), but as highly motivated, benign, facilitating, parent-friendly professionals. At the same time, pupil progress and achievement are measured in an increasingly rigid way, and teachers themselves are subject to scrutiny and judgement of a most impersonal and often punitive kind.

In the brief time since I wrote the paper that is reprinted here, it seems that extra layers of assessment and evaluation have been added in an attempt to "drive up standards". It becomes increasingly obvious that much of this is actually about keeping emotional experience *out* of the picture. This is in line with a political culture in which the response to any increase in antisocial behaviour (or social malaise such as the current prevalence of binge-drinking) is to install video cameras and introduce higher levels of policing and more severe penalties. There is little room for including thinking about the nature of human experience, let alone for reflection on the complexity of internal dynamics.

It is for this reason that I have chosen to include a final chapter (chapter 13) that focuses on aspects of inclusion and exclusion. Most of the characters who illustrate my arguments in this chapter will now be in their forties. Some may have grandchildren attending—or failing to attend—school. It was the challenging and puzzling behaviour of these adolescents that first led me to psychoanalytic thinking. I attended the Emotional Factors in Learning and Teaching course at the Tavistock in search of answers. I quickly learned that I would not be given *answers* but, instead, the opportunity to ask questions and to reflect on my observations (of myself as well as my pupils) in a way that opened up, for me, a new world of thinking and understanding. It seems fitting that these young people should find a place in this book.

Note

For the sake of confidentiality the names of all children have been changed. In non-specific instances, the masculine pronoun has been used for all children, and the feminine pronoun for all teachers.

CHAPTER ONE

"Where do babies come from?"
What makes children want to learn?

Hamish Canham

In this chapter, I want to consider what are the fundamental questions for those involved in the education of children and adolescents. What facilitates learning, and what hinders it? To what extent are difficulties in learning emotionally determined, and to what extent are they caused by external circumstances? Why do children find some subjects harder to learn than others? And the central question I want to address is—what makes children want to learn in the first place?

Difficulties in learning and thinking are central preoccupations for psychoanalysts and psychotherapists as well as for teachers. Melanie Klein's earliest publications were about children's difficulties in school and with learning, reading, and writing. Psychotherapists are interested in difficulties in learning and thinking because the ability to think about oneself and to learn from experience are crucial in the development of the personality and in the ability to make use of psychoanalytic treatment.

In the novel *Hard Times* (1854), Charles Dickens seems to be illustrating contrasting ways of learning (Canham & Youell, 2000). Mr M'Choakumchild and Mr Gradgrind teach a system of learning based on "facts" and the accumulation of knowledge in which the role of imagination or "fancy" is subordinated to the dry, meaningless repetition by rote of the external characteristics of objects. Sissy Jupe breathes life into learning through a meaningful, personal connection to the subject by using her mind and having independence of thought. The distinction that Dickens is making in the extract below would seem to correspond to that made by the psychoanalyst Wilfred Bion (1962), between "learning from experience" and "learning about"—a difference between amassing information "about" a subject without a genuine emotional link to what is being studied. It is the capacity to learn from experience with which I am primarily concerned here.

In *Hard Times*, Mr Gradgrind begins by outlining his educational philosophy to the schoolmaster, Mr M'Choakumchild, and then demonstrates it to the class:

> "Now, what I want is, Facts. Teach these boys and girls nothing but Facts. Facts alone are wanted in life. Plant nothing else, and root out everything else. You can only form the minds of reasoning animals upon Facts: nothing else will ever be of any service to them. This is the principle on which I bring up my own children and this is the principle on which I bring up these children. Stick to Facts, Sir!"
>
> "Now, let me ask you girls and boys, would you paper a room with representations of horses?" After a pause, one half of the children cried in chorus, "Yes, Sir!" Upon which the other half—seeing in the gentleman's face that Yes was wrong, cried out in chorus.
>
> "No, Sir!"—as the custom is in these examinations.
>
> "Of course, No. Why wouldn't you?"
>
> A pause. One corpulent, slow boy with a wheezy manner of breathing, ventured the answer, Because he wouldn't paper a room at all, but would paint it. "You must paper it," said Thomas Gradgrind, "whether you like it or not. Don't tell us you wouldn't paper it. What do you mean, boy?"
>
> "I'll explain to you then," said the gentleman, after another and dismal pause, "why you wouldn't paper a room with representations of horses. Do you ever see horses walking up and down the sides of rooms in reality—in fact? Do you?" "Yes, Sir!" from one half. "No, Sir!" from the other.

This stifling of imagination and conviction that there is a right way to view the world is, of course, represented in Mr M'Choakumchild's and Mr Gradgrind's names. Sissy—or Cecilia, as Mr Gradgrind calls her—has another view of things:

> There being a general conviction by this time that "No, Sir!" was always the right answer to this gentleman, the chorus of No was very strong. Only a few feeble stragglers said Yes; among them Sissy Jupe. "Girl number twenty," said the gentleman, smiling in the calm strength of knowledge. Sissy blushed, and stood up. "So you would carpet your room—or your husband's room if you were a grown woman, and had a husband—with representations of flowers, would you," said the gentleman. "Why would you?" "If you please, Sir, I am very fond of flowers," returned the girl. "And is that why you would put tables and chairs upon them, and have people walking over them in heavy boots?" "It wouldn't hurt them, Sir. They wouldn't crush and wither, if you please, Sir. They would be pictures of what was very pretty and pleasant and I would fancy—"
>
> "Ay, ay, ay! But you mustn't fancy," cried the gentleman, quite elated by coming so happily to his point. "That's it! You are never to fancy."
>
> "You are not, Cecilia Jupe," Thomas Gradgrind solemnly repeated, "to do anything of that kind."

I do not want to suggest that there is no place for facts and figures—and, indeed, for latency-age (primary school) children, acquiring this kind of knowledge serves important functions. But it is the capacity to learn from experience—the development in children of the ability to use their minds and to think and feel—that will help prepare them for life, and what I am referring to when I am talking about "learning".

Psychoanalytic theories of learning— the epistemophilic instinct

In her 1931 paper, "A Contribution to the Theory of Intellectual Inhibition", the psychoanalyst Melanie Klein proposed that every child is born with a desire to find out about the world, and she calls this "the epistemophilic instinct". In the earliest stages of life, she felt that this curiosity is focused on the mother and what is going on inside her. With time the scope of the child's curiosity grows to include other family members and the nature and quality of the relationship between these people and the mother. This initial interest in close family members gradually is turned towards the wider world and is the basis for the desire to learn.

I want to come later to the part played by the parents and other family members in fostering a desire to learn, and begin with the problem of the epistemophilic instinct—that children and adults may not like what they find out or innately know. There is a life-long struggle with which we are all faced, about what we can bear to learn and to know about. A tension between a desire to find out, and a desire not to know the truth. There is a problem at the heart of learning. New knowledge, or the acceptance of what we already know to be the truth deep down, often arouses angry opposition. As Britton (1992) writes, "It [new knowledge] arouses our hostility, threatens our security, challenges our claims to omniscience, reveals our ignorance and sense of helplessness and releases our latent hatred of all things new or foreign" (p. 38).

This was quite literally the case when Galileo claimed that the earth went round the sun, rather than vice versa. At the time he was forced to retract his claims, as it was felt by the religious and political figures of the time that to accept this heliocentric theory would completely undermine the structure upon which their world and domination of it was built—that God had created the universe and the solar system and that the earth and God's appointed representatives—the pope, the cardinals, the monarchy—were at the centre of it. I do think that it is important to bear in mind the kind of primitive reaction that new knowledge stirs up and to try to find ways of introducing ideas so that they can be heard and thought about rather than defended against and rejected as a consequence. Emily Dickinson's poem "Tell all the Truth but tell it slant" (1868) captures the nature of this dilemma:

Tell all the Truth but tell it slant—
Success in Circuit lies
Too fright for our infirm Delight
The Truth's superb surprise
As lightning to the Children eased
With explanation kind
The truth must dazzle gradually
Or every man be blind

In thinking about this problem, I have found the ideas of the psychoanalyst Roger Money-Kyrle particularly helpful. In his papers "Cognitive Development" (1968) and "The Aim of Psychoanalysis" (1971), he argues that there are three key facts of life and that the acceptance or disavowal of these enhances or impedes our ability to learn (see also Steiner, 1993, for a discussion of Money-Kyrle's idea). The first of these three facts of life is what he calls "the recognition of the breast as a supremely good object". This is his way of expressing the fact that, as babies, we are utterly dependent for survival on being looked after by someone else—generally our mothers. Without the care and attention of another person, a baby will very soon die.

The implications for this in the classroom are many. Children who cannot accept being dependent on someone outside themselves for survival are likely to have problems in accepting that they need the teacher's help to learn. They might present in class as children who cannot learn because they know it already, or who secretly take in what the teacher is saying without acknowledging where the learning is coming from. It is a type of learning that manifests itself in plagiarism—where the true originator of an idea is not acknowledged—or as a kind of "scavenging learning", as Meltzer and Harris (1986) call it, where a person puts together work by picking up bits and pieces from various sources and putting them together as if they were his or her own ideas. Accepting this fact of life is closely related to a child's disposition—whether he is able to tolerate frustration and gratefully take in what he is given, or whether he feels such envy of his mother's capacity to look after him and then of the teacher's capacities and knowledge that he attacks what is on offer.

The second of Money-Kyrle's facts of life is "the recognition of the parents' intercourse as a supremely creative act". In this way, Money-Kyrle introduces the centrality of the relationship between parents to mental life—the problems of the Oedipus complex. Melanie Klein thought that our ability to learn about the world and ourselves has its roots in the way a child discovers and approaches the nature of the relationship between parents and that many difficulties with learning in general follow on from difficulties in learning about the Oedipus situation. Seamus Heaney's poem *Death of a Naturalist* (1966) can, I think, be read as a description of a little boy's desire to find out about how babies are made and of the fine line between an ordinary curiosity about where babies come from and an intrusive interest that is more about taking over and controlling.

Death of a Naturalist

All year the flax-dam festered in the heart
Of the townland; green and heavy headed
Flax had rotted there, weighted down by huge sods.
Daily it sweltered in the punishing sun.
Bubbles gargled delicately, bluebottles
Wove a strong gauze of sound around the smell.
There were dragon-flies, spotted butterflies,
But best of all was the warm thick slobber
Of frogspawn that grew like clotted water
In the shade of the banks. Here, every spring
I would fill jampotfuls of the jellied
Specks to range on window-sills at home,
On shelves at school, and wait and watch until
The fattening dots burst into nimble-
Swimming tadpoles. Miss Walls would tell us how
The daddy frog was called a bullfrog
And how he croaked and how the mammy frog
Laid hundreds of little eggs and this was
Frogspawn. You could tell the weather by frogs too
For they were yellow in the sun and brown
In rain.

Then one hot day when fields were rank
With cowdung in the grass the angry frogs
Invaded the flax-dam; I ducked through hedges
To a coarse croaking that I had not heard
Before. The air was thick with a bass chorus.
Right down the dam gross-bellied frogs were cocked
On sods; their loose necks pulsed like sails. Some hopped:
The slap and plop were obscene threats. Some sat
Poised like mud grenades, their blunt heads fluting.
I sickened, turned, and ran. The great slime kings
Were gathered there for vengeance and I knew
That if I dipped my hand the spawn would clutch it.

The boy in the poem seems to have become frightened about what he has done—how he might have intruded into the parental intercourse by taking away the babies in the form of tadpoles. He seems to fear that the parents (the frogs) would want to attack him in return. The title of the poem, *Death of a Naturalist*, suggests that as an area of study, the natural world—perhaps biology in particular—has, as a result of the intrusiveness with which he has approached it, lost its interest for him and become something to be run away from instead.

I think there is often a more subtle turning away from recognizing this fact—that our parents have had a sexual relationship from which we are excluded. The widespread fantasy that many adults and children have at some point that they have been adopted and are in fact the lost offspring of royalty (what Freud, 1909c, called a "family romance") is one example. You can see how the evasion of knowing this fact of life can have implications for learning in the classroom. Most obviously, difficulties in learning about biology may be rooted in this. But so, too, might be difficulties in other subject areas like maths. Although this might seem like an unlikely jump, the connection was illustrated to me by a 6-year-old patient of mine whom I shall call Anna.

This girl's parents, while both involved in her upbringing, separated soon after the birth of her younger sibling. They remain close and are thinking of getting back together again. In the session I am going to describe, for the first time in about a year both parents had brought her together for her session. Usually the mother brought the girl for her sessions, occasionally the father.

Anna comes into the room and she begins drawing faces on a piece of paper. She first draws her face, then mine, then her father's, then her sister's. Finally she draws her mother's face. It is as far away from her father's as it is possible to be on the paper, and it is also drawn very small indeed. All the other faces are drawn in the space between her mother's and father's. Anna then draws arrows linking everybody, all possible relationships except that between her mother and father. I talk to Anna about how difficult she seems to find it to think of her mother and father being together, and both bringing her for her session today. I point out that in fact she seems to want to keep them apart, as she has drawn them on opposite sides of the paper, and they are the only people not joined by arrows. Anna then decides to do some maths, which she has begun to learn about at school. She gets another piece of paper and writes out some sums for herself, 1 + 46, and writes the answer = 46. The next sum is 10 + 18, and the answer she writes is 18.

So one can see how Anna's difficulties with seeing her parents together means she has similar difficulties with her maths. She can only see half of the sum. Bringing together 1 and 46, or 10 and 18, means allowing her parents to have a relationship with one another and to come together in her mind. In this example, there is an interplay of external and internal factors that makes it hard for Anna to see her parents as a couple. They are in reality separated, but in her mind she separates them further. I have given more space to this fact of life and called this paper "Where Do Babies Come From?" because of the central role that negotiating the Oedipus complex has in relation to the development of the personality and the ability to learn.

The third and last of Money-Kyrle's facts of life is "the recognition of the inevitability of time, and ultimately death". Recognition of this fact is connected very much to the experience of weaning, as the prototype for all subsequent losses. As Steiner (1993) comments:

> It is connected with the recognition of the fact that all good things have to come to an end, and it is precisely this fact that access to the breast cannot go on forever that makes us aware of the reality of its existence in the external world. [p. 99]

In the classroom, this may manifest itself as a difficulty with supply teachers or in moving from one subject or classroom to another. It may mean a difficulty with accepting the reality of time, which means that children or teenagers hand in homework late or do not leave sufficient time for getting it done or for exam revision. The origin of all these linked difficulties can be said to lie in an evasion of the reality that time is limited. It is perhaps most pronounced as a state of mind developmentally in adolescence, when there can be a sense that time is theirs to play with endlessly. However, as Eliot Jaques (1965) has pointed out in his paper "Death and the Mid-Life Crisis", the inevitability of death is something that needs to be revisited, particularly in middle age, in order to ensure the continued development of the character and capacity for work and love.

These facts of life can serve as both as a spur or obstacle to learning and, more often, as an oscillating combination of the two in which the desire to face reality and know the truth vies with the part of the personality that does not want to know. However, which character aspect, or part of the personality, holds sway for the majority of time will be determined not just by the individual character endowment of the child, but by the experience of learning in the earliest mother–infant and family–infant interactions.

Learning in infancy

Extending the theories of Klein, Bion (1962) put forward a model of learning based on the pattern of interaction between mother and baby in the earliest stages of the relationship. He suggested that when babies are very small, they need substantial help from their mothers in thinking about and making sense of their experiences of the world. If a baby has an experience of an adult who can "contain" the primitive anxieties communicated by their babies, he has the experience of being thought about. If this experience is a relatively consistent one, then when he needs to think for himself he is likely to be able to draw on the memory of this when less dependent on the actual physical and mental presence of the mother. Being able to learn and think has its roots, therefore, in a meeting of minds between mother and baby. Although it is generally the mother who performs this function, it should be stressed that it can be performed by any attuned carer.

The way in which parents and babies come together in the earliest months of life and negotiate a feeding relationship sets the scene for all subsequent experiences. Feeding—taking in food, digesting it, sorting out what is good from what is bad—is the prototype for learning. Our language is full of references to this link—"read, learn, and digest", "chew it over", "hungry for knowledge", and so forth. And so a model of learning based on learning from experience, of being able to sustain interest and curiosity, is built up inside the child.

The outcome of the meeting of minds in Bion's theory of container–contained is not simply a function of the mother's receptiveness, capacity to tolerate anxiety, and thoughtfulness. Each baby is born with a different disposition, envy, hostility, passivity, and so on, which influences the experience of being thought about for both mother and child. There is, right from the beginning of life, a complicated intermingling of individual nature with external experience. As a child grows older, it will be this sense of being accompanied in the task of learning that helps the child. The younger the child is, the more this accompanying will depend on the actual physical presence of a parent or another adult—a nursery worker or teacher, for instance. Although I think a sense of internal company can make itself felt from a young age, small children do need a lot of help with learning. And I think this is for two main reasons.

First, small children need someone to share with them the pleasure in finding out about the world. When a toddler learns how to do something new, very often the first reaction is to want to share this discovery with his parents or carer. Naturally if the child feels that this pleasure in making a discovery is matched by a pleasure in the parents (or teachers etc.) at what the child is learning, then he will be encouraged to go on discovering. When talking with parents of young children, I have been struck by how they comment on viewing the world from a new angle—through the eyes of their children—which helps them to rediscover feelings and thoughts from their own childhoods or makes them see things in a new light. In this atmosphere, I think children feel they are on a shared learning experience in which the parents are learning alongside the child. I suppose this is true at a more profound level, in that parents (and teachers) are learning how to parent this particular child. However experienced as parents, teachers, therapists we are, each encounter with a new child means thinking about what we are doing in relation to the particular personality of this child.

Second, I think small children need help with learning because of the levels of anxiety that it stirs up, and this is one of the reasons why the issue of classroom size is so important. If learning can happen within a relatively intimate setting, then the potential for containing anxiety about not knowing, feeling small, feeling stupid, feeling competitive, and so on is much greater. As children grow they become more reliant on their peers to perform some of these functions, but, again, children and adolescents are profoundly affected in their capacity to learn by whether the prevailing ethos in the group is pro- or anti-learning.

Difficulties in learning

It is when there is a protracted difficulty in making a link between mother and baby that there are likely to be consequences for the child in being able to learn. This is most starkly shown in cases where there is neglect and abuse.

Children who have experienced really inadequate containment do not introject parental figures interested in them and their development. Rather, they grow up feeling that people do not like them and have no time for them. They get overcome by feeling states that they are unable to process without a great deal of help, and the world becomes a frightening and bewildering place. In the face of overwhelming feelings such as these, children erect defensive structures to protect themselves. However, often these defensive structures impede learning as well as protecting against anxiety. Children like this can often seem aloof and disinterested in learning—constantly forgetting books, homework, even ideas. They will continually rub out or throw away work. These might all reflect an experience of feeling or being forgotten, perhaps feeling unwanted to the point of seeing themselves as rubbish. This feeling is often projected into teachers, who are seen as useless and therefore as having nothing to teach.

This is the tragedy of deprivation. The initial deprivation of not being thought about means that the person then deprives him/herself again of the opportunity for help and learning. So, in each new situation, the original one gets re-evoked. This is what Williams (1997) calls "double deprivation". The point I am making is that an early experience of deprivation sets up a vicious circle in which children find learning very hard. The opposite is also true—that a child with good early experiences will generally approach the teacher and the task of learning with a positive expectation. Children who have been traumatized or abused often stop viewing the world as an essentially benevolent place full of interesting things to be discovered but, rather, feel it is full of potential persecutors against which they need to protect themselves. Crucial to how children recover from traumatic experiences and abuse is the capacity of the surrounding adults to help them process the trauma—that is, to help the children to think about what has happened, however difficult this might at first seem. In this way, children and adolescents see that thinking and learning can continue, however painful the struggle might feel. There are some situations in which the parental capacity to help the child think is tested to the limits.

I recently heard about a 10-year-old girl who was having terrible difficulties in school with reading and writing and with understanding what she was asked to do. During the course of an exploratory interview with this girl's mother, it emerged that several years previously, when the girl was about 6, she had discovered her father dead following an overdose. The body was quickly removed, and this girl was told for several months that her father was unwell in hospital. Immediately after her husband's suicide the mother was overwhelmed with grief and guilt, found it hard to make sense of the experience for herself, and could not find a way of telling her daughter what had happened. The girl was left in a very confused state for quite a while, in which part of her clearly knew that her father was dead, having discovered the body (and, it subsequently transpired, overheard conversations about him being dead), yet another part of her mind really wanted to believe that he was only in hospital and was still alive. This bit of her was encouraged, so to speak, by her mother, who in the immediate period afterwards could not help her daughter to bear the truth of what she already knew.

This is an extreme example, but I think it points to the importance of parents, and other adults, helping children find a way to the truth. Bion's version of the epistemophilic instinct is that we are all born with the desire to find out the truth about the world—he felt that truth is to the mind what food is to the body, and therefore, conversely, lies or distortions of the truth poison our minds. Of course, with children especially, there are always judgements to be made about what they are ready to know or how much it is appropriate for them to be told at a particular stage of development.

I think there are opportunities for teachers and therapists working with individual and groups of children to provide something different—to offer to children and adolescents the model of trying to think about things even if this does stir up feelings of uncertainty, ignorance, and irritability. There are, therefore, always opportunities for coming into contact with a new way of learning that can tap into the fundamental desire to find out the truth about the world.

I want, finally, to make the point that this is not just down to individual teachers. The whole way that a school, as an organizational system, functions is fundamentally important to the type of learning encouraged in its pupils. School, perhaps more than other organizations, has to demonstrate to the pupils a capacity to learn. By this I mean that if the pupils see and have the experience of a place where the staff talk to one another and take seriously issues raised by pupils, somewhere that goes on evolving in the face of new challenges both from within and outside the school, then they have a very solid containing structure around them as a model of how learning from experience can function.

CHAPTER TWO

A theoretical overview: an introduction to psychoanalytic concepts and their application

The relationship between learning and anxiety

Sigmund Freud's conceptualization of the unconscious within the mind provides a model for distinguishing between conscious, logical processes and the irrational, unconscious forces that drive much of human behaviour. Through his clinical practice and analysis of his own dream life, he came to understand that unconscious phantasy seemed to be related to very early experience and infantile wishes. Freud also discovered that sexuality played a huge role in the infantile parts of the mind, and he became particularly interested in the way young children have powerful phantasies of being in sole possession of one or other parent (the oedipal situation). His case study of Little Hans (Freud, 1909b), the 5-year-old son of one of his colleagues, showed the way in which the passionate desire to possess one parent involves hatred for the other and brings with it tremendous anxiety, guilt, and fear of punishment. Freud continued to develop his model of the mind, and by the 1930s he had located the first experience of life-threatening anxiety as the first experience of separation—separation from the mother at birth.

Melanie Klein was the first psychoanalyst to work directly with child patients. Freud had established "free association" and the analysis of dreams as key clinical techniques, and Mrs Klein argued that children's play and drawings could be observed and interpreted in the same way. Her development of Freudian theory holds that the greatest spur to learning is the anxiety associated with separation from the feeding breast (mother or caregiver). The infant has good experiences of feeling comfortable and well fed and comes to associate this feeling state with the mother's care (the "good breast"). Mrs Klein suggests that the infant employs splitting in order to preserve the "good" satisfying mother who is loved from the absent or frustrating mother who is hated (the "bad breast"). These are first seen as entirely separate entities, but over time the child comes to understand that the mother who sometimes fails to make him comfortable is actually one and the same person as the mother who attends lovingly to his needs. In this way, the split comes together, the infant learns to tolerate the frustration of waiting and to bear ambivalent feelings: the mother is both the loved and the hated object.

This development is what Mrs Klein described as the "depressive position", a state of mind in which there is recognition of the separateness of the other and the beginnings of altruistic concern. This is in contrast to what she called the paranoid-schizoid position, in which splitting and projection predominate. These terms are used to describe not a linear development, but two states of mind between which we oscillate throughout life. Put simply, in a paranoid-schizoid state of mind, anxiety is high and thinking is difficult, whereas in the depressive position, anxiety is manageable and there is mental space for taking in new experiences, for learning. A paranoid-schizoid state of mind implies that there is excessive envy and lack of trust, whereas the depressive position implies concern and gratitude.

After Melanie Klein, Wilfred Bion (1961) developed his theory of "container–contained" in the mother–infant relationship and linked this with the origins of thinking and the capacity to learn. He proposed that it is the mother's job to make sense of the bewildering sensations that bombard the baby in the early hours, days, and weeks of life. For a baby, the world is a place full of smells, noises, lights, shadows as well as ill-defined internal feelings of comfort, pleasure, discomfort, and so on. The mother attempts to meet the baby's needs and, through trial and error, gets it right some of the time. She is thinking about what the baby might be feeling and is open to unconscious communication (projections) from the baby. A mother who is attuned comes to recognize a particular kind of cry as indicating hunger, another as indicative of discomfort or a need to be held. In this way, over time, the baby has repeated experiences of being thought about and understood. Feelings are connected up, for him, with thoughts in his mother's mind, and this, in turn, helps him to make sense of his experiences. If all goes well, or well enough, the baby begins to take in (introject) the experience of being thought about and understood, which will form the basis for the development of a capacity to think.

With the introjection of good, sustaining experiences comes the establishing of good internal objects. Although different in some important details, the idea of a good internal object has much in common with notions of resilience, secure attachment, strong sense of identity, and self-esteem. It suggests that there is a solid core of the personality, that the child is developing inner resources to call upon in the face of future challenges. Both Klein and Bion wrote about the way in which the absence of this kind of experience leaves the infant vulnerable to feelings of primitive anxiety, what Esther Bick (1986) describes as "the catastrophic anxieties of the dead-end, falling through space, liquefying, life-spilling-out variety . . ." (p. 71).

An extract from an observation of a young baby may illustrate some of the points made so far. The account is written by a student who was embarking on the psychoanalytic observational studies course at the Tavistock Clinic. As part of this course, weekly visits are made to observe a developing baby from birth to 2 years old.

Lauren was 4 weeks old at the time of this observation. She had three older siblings, and the family had just returned from the "school run" at the end of the afternoon. Lauren's eldest brother (William, aged 10 years) was holding her while their mother quickly took shopping through to the kitchen and began supper preparations.

William sat on the sofa with his baby sister on his lap. He took care to place her on her back, stretched out along his thighs in the way he had seen his mother do many times. Lauren looked up into William's face and seemed settled. After a moment of quietness, Lauren's face crumpled and she let out a little cry. She began to go red in the face, and William looked anxious. He lifted and turned the baby so that she was up against his shoulder. Lauren liked this even less and began to grumble. Her feet were rather twisted and crushed against her brother's chest, and her face began to contort in real discomfort. William put her down on her back on the sofa and tried to talk to her, but he had lost confidence and he called out to his mother. As if detecting the rising panic in William's voice, Lauren let out a piercing scream. Her body was rigid and her clenched fists were shaking as her feet kicked at the air. Her mother came in and scooped her up, thanking William and saying that Lauren was tired and she would put her down. I [the observer] followed her, and she was saying softly that Lauren could rest in the dining-room, away from the noisy TV.

Lauren continued to scream angrily, and mother sighed as she told me that Lauren had been very tolerant but she knew she had expected too much of her. She walked back and forth, holding her against her shoulder and rocking her gently. I thought the mother looked exhausted and much more anxious than usual. However, Lauren did quieten down eventually, and as the mother settled her into the cot, she told her sympathetically that it was tough being a fourth baby—the world doesn't revolve around you and you just have to fit in. She stroked her cheeks and kissed the back of her head before pulling the covers over her and telling her she could have a sleep now. She left the baby and went over to the kitchen area.

Lauren was still for a moment but, as soon as she had gone away, began to stir a little. When her mother spoke to me, Lauren opened her eyes wide and turned her head towards the kitchen. She began to stretch and kick and then to grumble. Her face became red as her grumbles developed into full cries. Her mother called out her name and said she was coming and then came over and looked down, saying Lauren might just settle if she left her, but almost immediately saying that she didn't think she would. She lifted her out of the cot and sat down, laying her on her knees so that she could look up at her. She talked to her soothingly. "Yes, that's what you wanted isn't it? Just a bit of peace and quiet after your busy afternoon. You just wanted to be held."

Lauren was quiet immediately and seemed to be staring into her eyes as she continued to talk to her about all the things they had been doing. After a few minutes, she offered her the breast. She took it and began to suck enthusiastically.

In this brief extract we see a baby's experience of alternating comfort and discomfort and her mother's attempts to understand her experience as well as to manage the ordinary demands of family life. We see the way in which the baby's distress is experienced by her brother and the escalating panic in both of them before their mother intervenes. She is careful to thank William for his efforts before turning her mind fully to her baby.

It is undoubtedly the case that some individuals make better parents than others and that some babies are easier to care for than others. Failures in the container–contained relationship can come about for any number of reasons. Bion (1962) takes his theory further by suggesting that when a mother cannot process her baby's projections, the baby is subject to a double dose of anxiety. He has an experience of not being understood, and his projections come back at him with added toxicity, loaded as they are with his mother's conscious or unconscious distress and frustration. This happens occasionally in every baby's life but is, of course, likely to be a much more frequent occurrence if a baby is innately more difficult to feed or comfort, or if a mother is over-anxious, under pressure, or depressed.

The idea of containment and good internal objects can be misleading when it is made to sound like some kind of magical process that inoculates the growing child against mental pain and struggle. It does not work this way. Anxiety is an unavoidable part of learning and development throughout the life cycle. Indeed, it can be argued that without a measure of anxiety, there can be no learning. At the very least, there has to be recognition of a state of "not knowing", with the accompanying anxiety, before learning can take place. Part of this is allowing for the fact that somebody else knows what we do not. Where there is excessive envy and a denial of dependency, this simple reality may be experienced as highly persecutory (see chapter 1).

Defences against anxiety

It has long been recognized that human beings need ways in which to defend themselves against the full impact of primitive anxiety. Not all defences are anti-developmental or pathological. It is now commonplace to talk in terms of "healthy" or "necessary" splitting and about the positive use of projective identification. Defences against anxiety become destructive forces in development and learning when they are used to excess and when they remain unconscious, unavailable to thought and therefore not available for modification.

To return to the prototypical experiences of very early life, I shall draw briefly on three infant observations that serve to illustrate the way in which individuals develop different preferences or styles in defending themselves against anxiety. The external picture was similar in each of the observations. The babies were all girls, all born of older parents with doting grandparents and all facing the changes associated with weaning. In all three cases, the weaning was happening because the mothers were returning to work. The first baby, Charlotte, was reacting in an aggressive way: spitting out food, biting her mother, and letting out a piercingly angry scream whenever her father approached her. Her family were astonished by the strength of her protest. The second baby, Stephanie, by contrast, made no protest but was forging ahead in her development. She and her parents seemed to have come to a tacit agreement that the best response to this new situation was to focus on learning new skills. Her grandparents bought her challenging toys, and all the adults joined in celebrating her achievements. It could be said that she was being given new "food" and was devouring it. The third baby, Angela, reacted by becoming physically active, almost permanently on the move. She developed a speedy, muscular crawl and moved about the flat non-stop. She was undeterred by tumbles or by collisions with furniture. This physical defence seemed to the observer to be the baby's way of trying to manage her mother's unexplained disappearance—perhaps even to become mobile enough to go after her. The observer had been distressed to see Angela's father turning the baby's face to the wall so that her mother could slip out behind her back.

In each of the three cases, it could be argued that the external change—the mother returning to work and the associated weaning from the breast—was a spur to the girl's development. The three responses were different but within a normal range. It is perhaps interesting to speculate as to what may be the learning styles of these three girls when at school and what kinds of defences they will resort to in the face of extreme anxiety. Will Stephanie continue to "devour" new learning, and will this be at the expense of other aspects of development? Will Charlotte protest vociferously when life seems cruel and unfair, and will Angela continue to make use of physical activity to keep anxious feelings at bay?

It is important to stress that these observations are interesting but not unusual. All babies and young children develop ways to manage their anxiety, and traces of these early mechanisms are likely to remain in later developmental phases, particularly in relation to the challenges presented by formal education. However, it is also important to stress that defensive structures of this kind are not immutable. They can be challenged and modified by flexible, responsive parenting and, later, by containing school experience.

Mrs Bick (1968) made a very important contribution to psychoanalytic understanding of the development of defences when she wrote about the ways in which infants develop a "second skin", a psychic equivalent of the bodily skin which gives the baby its first experience of being held together. In her seminal papers (1968, 1986), she gives examples of ways in which infants hold themselves together in very early life: by staring at a light or fixing their attention on a noise, by sucking or fingering a favoured object. Her notion is that the infant creates an illusion of being "held" by latching on in this way and that, in later development, this defensive mechanism takes the form of what she calls "adhesive identification". This has particular relevance to thinking about models of learning, since the "adhesive" defence is recognizable in children whose learning is restricted to the imitative. These are the children who cling to the teacher or to their peers in what can feel like a cloying, claustrophobic way and whose preference is often for repetitive exercises and for accurate copying rather than free expression in drawing, writing, or stories.

Trauma, deprivation, and abuse

As Hamish indicates in the previous chapter, the relationship between the external world and internal development is very clearly seen where there has been actual trauma, deprivation, or abuse in early life. He refers to Gianna Williams's invaluable contribution in her paper "Double Deprivation" (1997), which sets out the ways in which the capacity to make use of developmental opportunities (educational and therapeutic) is compromised by an internal world that is populated by malign objects. This is a very important consideration for all who are seeking to support the development of children and young people who have suffered actual traumatic experiences.

The teacher and school as container

It has often been suggested (Orford, 1996; Salzberger-Wittenberg, Henry, & Osborne, 1983) that when the child moves into formal education, the teacher and the school take over the role of containing "parent". The challenge that schools face is how to harness anxiety in the interests of learning and creativity. How can the school ensure that levels of anxiety are manageable and do not spiral out of control—either on an individual level or on an institutional level? How, in other words, does the school achieve the kind of containment described above?

Salzberger-Wittenberg (1970) writes helpfully about the process of containment in professional relationships. She is describing social workers and their clients, but the process applies just as accurately to teachers and their pupils:

> The caseworker may not be able to pick up the most pressing anxieties of the client at any particular moment of time. What is essential to the client is the caseworker's willingness to try to understand how he feels, to be prepared to listen and respect

him as a unique personality. Her actions, as well as her words, will show whether she is really concerned about him and in touch with the adult and infantile parts of his personality and whether she has the courage and integrity to face the emotional pain. [p. 163]

The key here, in my view, is in the phrase "whether she has the courage and integrity to face the emotional pain". The social worker/teacher needs to be open to the client/child's unconscious as well as his conscious communication and to be able to bring thought to bear on the experience.

In Bion's formulation of container–contained, the baby communicates its state to the mother by projection. Not even the most sceptical of persons would argue with the idea that feeling states are communicated in ways other than with words and gestures. Teachers will all have had the experience of coming away from a class or an interaction with an individual pupil or parent, with feelings that they know are not their own—or, at least, that they did not have beforehand. They can be unaccountably angry, jittery and upset, bored and tired, or feeling a total failure. These are feelings that have been projected into them by others and have found a willing home. What they then do with them is the issue. If they are able to think about them and recognize them for what they are, they are halfway to being able to contain them in the sense described above. If they are not aware of the mechanism or have been observing with mind and feelings switched off, they may feel overwhelmed and unable to think and may then act out in very unhelpful ways.

A striking example of this took place in a secondary school on a Monday morning. The deputy head teacher arrived late to the morning staff briefing because he had been taking a call from the Local Authority. He was angry because the head teacher was off sick again, and he started the meeting with a list of criticisms of the staff. He complained about the untidiness of their classrooms, the untidiness of their car parking, the filth on the staffroom coffee cups, as well as about the exam results due that day, which he was sure would be appalling. The staff appeared to be absorbing all this without reacting. However, when the bell rang, everybody rushed for the door, almost pushing each other aside in their desire to break free. One teacher spotted a group of pupils leaning on the wall down the corridor: "Come here you animals! Stand up straight when I'm talking to you. Where's your tie, boy!" The un-contained feelings had simply been passed on down the line, from absent head to deputy, from deputy to staff, from staff to pupils. It seemed likely that the group of adolescents who had been shouted at would go in search of someone younger, smaller, or weaker to pass on the abuse.

Splitting: idealization and denigration

The way in which the infant employs splitting to protect his early good experiences from contamination is described by Hamish in the previous chapter and again in my description of early devel-opment above. It is however, a phenomenon that recurs in later development and throughout the life cycle. Very concrete splits can occur in a school setting, with pupils idealizing one teacher at the expense of another. All that is good is invested in the loved teacher, and all that is bad is projected into the hated teacher. It is, of course, very flattering to be the idealized teacher and very painful to be the denigrated one. Many find idealization irresistible, unwittingly playing into the split by believing in their own superiority. Howev-er, it usually becomes an uncomfortable position, as the unrealistic expectations begin to weigh heavy on the preferred teacher, who becomes anxious about crashing down to earth from their elevated position. This kind of splitting may replicate what happens in the child's family with the parents being split, whether it be by an oedipal toddler or a rampaging adolescent. What is often needed in school is just the same as is needed in family life—for the adults to get together and help the child to achieve a more realistic picture of both halves of the "parental" couple.

Splitting also occurs in schools in relation to subject areas, abil-ity groupings, staff seniority, management roles, and so forth. All of this has enormous impact on the way in which teachers view themselves and how they, in turn, split off and project aspects of their own unwanted emotional experience. This is explored in more detail in subsequent chapters, particularly, perhaps, in relation to the formalized processes of assessment and evaluation (chapter 12).

Defences against anxiety

Everybody has ways of defending him/herself against mental pain. All children, but particularly those who stand out from the crowd by virtue of their particular needs, have highly developed mechanisms for making sure that *they* do not feel stupid or inadequate. One such mechanism is to split off the bad feelings and project them into somebody else—"He's really stupid", "He's mad", and so on. Another version of the split is for the child to own all the stupidity himself and place all the competence in others. These are distressing children to work with, those who insist "I'm worthless. My work's rubbish. You shouldn't waste your time on me."

Some children, and adults, behave in a manic way to escape uncomfortable feelings; others withdraw or absent themselves. In some individuals, the mental or emotional pain will manifest itself in physical symptoms, chronic or repetitive ailments, or sudden accident-proneness. Adolescents may turn to delinquent acting out or escape through drink and drugs. Younger children may wet themselves, soil, cry, steal, or bully. One of the most common forms of defence, particularly in latency children, is that of omnipotence or omniscience. The child simply knows and can do everything. If he does not actually do the work, it is because it is stupid, boring, or too easy. For many of these children, the experience of "not knowing" is thought to be so dangerous and unbearable that the risk is never taken. These are the children who truly cannot learn until they have had sufficient containment to take the risk of letting go of the omnipotence, to bear not knowing, and to allow the knowledge to exist in another (the teacher). If this does not happen in early childhood or latency, the teacher will probably be faced with an adolescent who becomes confrontational at the very suggestion that he should focus on a piece of work. He has to believe that it is too easy for him; he cannot take the risk of trying and failing. If envy is the dominant force in the internal world, the child may have a phantasy that he has acquired the new knowledge or skill by theft and may be very fearful of being found out or of retaliation.

Countertransference

The way in which we recognize and think about what may have been projected into us is known, in clinical work, as *countertransference*. We pay attention to how we are feeling and think about whether it is an unconscious communication from the patient. This requires that one knows oneself well enough to be able to recognize what is one's own "emotional baggage". The capacity to examine one's responses in this way is what distinguishes "psychoanalytically" informed observation from other methods of watching, listening, and reflecting (chapter 7). Being able to think about their own emotional experience as well as that of their pupils is something that is of enormous importance in teachers' struggle to understand the children they are teaching, particularly those who worry or challenge them in some way.

Transference

Having referred to countertransference, I should say a little about its predecessor, in terms of the history of psychoanalytic thinking—the transference. This is the phenomenon that Freud first identified and named. He was struck by the way his patients developed feelings for him. At first he saw this as an irritation, an interference in the work, and an obstacle to the patient's recovery. Later, he began to realize that it was something important to take into account. He began to see that the patients were bringing their own emotional histories with them into the consulting-room and were experiencing him *as if* he were a potential lover, a devoted father, a punitive rabbi, or whatever figure fitted with their own particular internal world-view. Towards the end of his working life, he incorporated this understanding into his clinical practice, always thinking about what was being attributed to him "in the transference". Teachers are very familiar with being treated in ways that do not seem at all consistent with how they view themselves. They know they have been fair but are accused of gross injustice. They believe themselves to be relaxed and patient but are experienced as short tempered and moany.

This phenomenon is clear for all to see in young children. Moving from their primary caregiver to a new adult, children—who are much less inhibited than adults—often start by calling the new person "Mummy". When a child slips up and calls a teacher "Mummy", it does not necessarily mean that the child is immature. On the contrary, it may indicate that he has an idea of a good, safe, parent figure and he knows what he wants or needs at that moment. Although older children soon learn not to make this kind of slip, the transference to teacher as a parent figure can persist throughout school life and will become very significant at times of particular stress or anxiety, such as on school outings or when examinations are taking place.

Away in the mountains on an outdoor-activities trip, a group of very streetwise city truants insisted on calling their teachers "Mummy" and "Daddy". Each night they went through the "Waltons'" (idealized American TV soap, featuring a family of seven children) family ritual of saying goodnight to "the parents" and to each other: "Goodnight Jim Bob, goodnight Mary Ellen . . . goodnight Mummy, goodnight Daddy, goodnight Grandpa. Goodnight children, go to sleep now. Goodnight Everybody." They did this with heavy sarcasm, but it was clearly their way of expressing just how far away from home they felt (most had never before been out of London) and how much they depended on the staff to be competent adults. When they arrived back in London at the end of the week and were dropped off in their neighbourhood, they treated the teachers like the abandoning parents they felt them to be. They left the minibus swearing, farting loudly, giggling, and spitting into the gutter. The holiday, they insisted, had been "rubbish", and they were glad to be back. The loss of the containment of the "family" group could not be faced but had to be denied through massive splitting and projection. The teachers were the ones to go home carrying the sense of loss and failure, feeling like "rubbish".

Roles and boundaries

The painful experience described above raises a number of challenging questions about how teachers manage their roles and what boundaries need to be kept in place. Would the teachers have been well-advised not to take the young people on such an expedition, or could it have been managed in a different way so that the emotional experience could have been better digested before the group disbanded? I am inclined towards the latter view. It would be very depressing to suggest that a teacher's role cannot extend beyond the school building—and, indeed, the holiday was a very significant "therapeutic" experience for the group. However, had the teachers been aware of the unconscious dynamics, they might have been more prepared for the attack that came at the moment of separation and might have been able to help their students to manage it in a different way.

One of this same group later took his teacher to task as she was organizing a new seating area in the off-site unit, setting out a new rug and comfortable chairs. He stormed out of the room, shouting "Stop it! It's not fair to make it like a home!" He later came back and settled into the new chairs as if his outburst had not happened. However, the message was a clear one. He needed his teachers to realize that school may offer some nurturing experiences but is not actually a home and that a teacher is a parental figure "in the transference" but remains a teacher with a particular role to play.

CHAPTER THREE

Play, playfulness, and learning

Twenty-first-century European society maintains a clear distinction between what is described as work and what is described as play. Although it is acknowledged that some people are fortunate enough to enjoy their work, work is most often represented as an unavoidable necessity. Play is seen as compensation, a reward. Schools promote this view from the earliest years when children are encouraged to earn "golden time" (play) by hard work and good behaviour. Bad behaviour or poor work is punished by the loss of playtime and the imposition of extra work. In a system that purports to promote positive attitudes to learning and education, we all too easily create structures that reinforce an idea that work is hard, if not actually unpleasant.

No such division exists in the mind of the young child. For the baby and toddler, play is work. It is the means by which he finds out about his surroundings and about the people he encounters. Interactions between mothers (or primary carers) and infants are characterized by playfulness. Mothers smile, tickle, and talk to their babies, and babies learn to respond with gurgles and smiles. "Games" and "jokes" (often involving noses, ears, or tummies) develop between them as a vocabulary of play is established long before the introduction of toys and long before language develops.

Learning and playing are inextricably linked, as the following extracts from an observation may serve to illustrate.

Timothy was 10 months old at the time of this extract. He had been sitting on the floor while his two older brothers watched TV and played around with a recorder. When their mother came in, they asked permission to go out to the park and then rushed past their baby brother, who looked very put out at being left behind. His mother spotted the look and invited him to come to her.

Timothy climbed onto his mother's lap, grinning as she pulled him towards her for a cuddle. He wriggled free and down onto the floor again. He reached out for the red plastic recorder his brother had dropped. He looked at it closely and tried various bits of it in his mouth before dropping it and going instead for a plastic rattle and a card baby-book. He took each in turn and examined it in detail before tossing them up in the air, his arms flapping forcefully against his sides. He played contentedly for a few moments before noticing that his mother was absentmindedly fingering the recorder. Seeing that he was looking at her, she put it to her mouth and played a single note. Timothy smiled with pleasure and reached out for the instrument. His mother gave it to him and he put it to his mouth, exploring both ends and the rounded surface in between. A few moments later, the recorder made a clear sound. Timothy pulled it away from his mouth, looking startled, and his face began to crumple. Then he looked towards his mother, who was exclaiming that he had played a note, and his face broke into a huge smile. He put the mouthpiece back in his mouth and repeated the performance. He was soon filling his cheeks with air before blowing, and the sounds were getting longer and louder. His mother was delighted and congratulated him, commenting that he was blowing deliberately—he had learned what to do. She didn't think either of his older brothers could have done the same at that age. Timothy was enjoying himself but after a while seemed to become aware that his achievement was no longer a cause for celebration, and he went over to the bookshelf. He reached towards the books and then paused, looking over his shoulder at his mother before putting just one finger on a book, grinning provocatively. She said "no" quite firmly, but his grin was infectious and she was soon smiling too. She repeated her command, and he continued to grin at her, now spreading two hands across the books on the top shelf. He looked as if he would pull the books down in spite of her, and I felt I had become part of his audience. I looked away to hide my amusement, and his mother managed to use a tone of voice that he understood really was a "no", and then she distracted him with another game.

The links with learning are clear in this sequence of play. Timothy is learning a skill by imitation and trial and error but is not doing so in isolation. He is confident that his mother is aware of what he is doing and that he can engage her interest when he needs to do so. This is reinforced by her response to his making a sound with the recorder. He had been watching with wrapt attention while his older brothers were playing the instrument and was spurred on by a real desire to do what they could do. He is delighted by the praise he receives, and this sustains him for a few minutes while he consolidates the learning by repetition. When he begins to feel alone with his play, he finds another way to engage his mother, and there is a playful interaction over his threat to pull down the books. This ends in his having to accept (learn) that she is the one who makes the rules and that he can only go so far with his provocation.

Two further extracts from the same observation will introduce ideas about the development of symbolic play and the importance of this in learning. The first extract is from an observation at nearly nine months, a few weeks before his encounter with the recorder.

Timothy 36 weeks. His mother pulled the baby-gym frame close to him, and I commented on how many stages I had witnessed him going through with this particular toy. At the beginning, he had lain under it, staring at it and flapping his hands, barely able to reach the dangling figures. His mother came back from the cooker to watch him for a moment. He was now sitting, looking into a mirror on the end of one of the dangling straps. He took hold of two of the figures, bringing them to his mouth and chewing on them thoughtfully, looking slightly put out when one or other slipped from his grasp. He allowed the figures to swing free and then reached out for the most distant one, the monkey, turning it upside down and then returning it to its proper position. After a few minutes, he dropped down onto his back, kicked at the figures with a giggle of pleasure, and rolled over before reaching out for a different toy.

Here we see a healthy baby playing in the safety of his mother's presence. He has a familiar "favourite" toy within reach and seems very comfortable. The observer comments on the developments in his play with this toy, and his mother comes to watch for a moment or two. Timothy is in a new relationship to the toy now that he can sit alongside it, and this presents him with new opportunities. The observer knew that he was in the process of being weaned at this time, and in this context we can speculate about the symbolic meaning of the two toys being grasped and brought to his mouth, and his distress when one slips from his grasp.

Some seven months later, the observer had an opportunity to revisit this idea. The baby gym had just been returned after being on loan to a friend's baby.

Timothy (17 months) examined the toy carefully from a standing position, towering above it. He began to run through all the different actions. He made the wheels spin, the dangling toys swing, the squeakers squeak—all at the same time. He giggled with excitement and tried to climb onto one of the side struts, but the whole frame tilted and he jumped back. He then gripped the tubular frame and lifted the whole assembly off the ground, holding it up like a trophy. He turned to one of his toy-boxes and began to unpack it. He took out a yellow sponge ball and a string of teddy bears that used to hang on his rocker chair. After that came a transparent ball with bells inside it and a rattle toy, which he examined closely. I recognized these toys as being his earliest and very much the ones that used to surround him when he lay under the baby-gym. He gathered them up and stowed them under the frame, and I could not resist drawing his mother's attention to what he was doing. She said that it was probably coincidental; after all, he had seen the same toy in lots of people's houses. However, when she saw which toys he had selected, she agreed that the reappearance of the toy must have provoked some kind of memory of earlier times. As we stood watching, he dragged his most recent acquisition, his dumper truck, over to join the heap of toys under the frame.

He went out into the hall and came back with a sponge ball and picked up the other one from the heap of toys. He put them both on the seat of his chair and tried to climb up. One rolled off, and he picked it up and tried to climb up with it in his hand. He tried several times to get himself and the two balls onto the chair, but he could not manage it and eventually the chair toppled over. He picked it up and changed the game, rolling the balls one by one over the back of the chair. "Drop. Drop." He sat on the floor and trapped the balls between his knees.

In this observation, we see the way in which Timothy, now a toddler, recognizes an old toy and is able to make links in his mind to aspects of his own past experience. His play shows us his pleasure in his current physical prowess (towering over the toy and using all the bits at once) but also an impressive capacity to revisit aspects of his earlier development. His play with the two balls was reminiscent of his earlier play with the two dangling figures (now accompanied by language, "Drop. Drop"). And again we may speculate that there is a link in his mind to the loss of the breast.

Timothy provides a vivid example of the centrality of play in early life and the close links between play and learning, between play and the work of finding out about the world. He also provides us with evidence as to how play and learning happen within relationships. He seems to be a well-endowed child in terms of his natural energy and curiosity, but it is his relationship with his mother (and no doubt with his father and brothers) that provides the container and the impetus for his development.

The importance of intimate relationships in the development of play and learning is underlined in an observation of young children in an East African orphanage. Here a group of twenty-seven children live together in very deprived circumstances. There is one resident caregiver, a janitor, and two part-time members of staff. The children's ages range from a few weeks to 17 years. These observations were made by a visiting group, bringing toys and art materials for a newly appointed teacher.

For a while we observed the children playing on four robust tricycles which they pedalled at a ferocious speed around the rough ground, often several to a bike. They were skilful and remarkably strong and seemed to get a lot of pleasure from the activity and the sense of being so in control of something. If they fell off or crashed into each other, they paused for a moment and their faces crumpled but they did not seem to look for comfort from the adults; they simply got up and started again. It was also striking that they didn't seem to retaliate if they were knocked off, or protest too much if somebody grabbed their tricycle from them. The older boys played football over the heads of the children on tricycles, and the ball struck several children on the head without them seeming to notice.

A little later, we gathered the children together and told them that we had brought toys for them to play with. When we opened the sack of Duplo there was a scramble to pick up pieces, and many handfuls disappeared into pockets or gathered-up skirts. We felt a moment of panic as the children scattered with their booty, but we need not have worried. Within minutes they were all back within sight and each was sitting on the floor puzzling as to how the bits fitted together. Over a period of about half an hour, they came together into groups, pooling their Duplo pieces. There were striking differences in what they were able to do with the materials. Most of the children could do little more than hold onto the pieces, looking at them and sometimes putting two bits together or gathering a few pieces of like colour or size into a heap. Dawn, a blank-faced 11-year-old, made a tower out of her bricks. She did so with very little energy or visible pleasure. By contrast, her friend, Mary, was busy accumulating little figures and then arranged them in a line, a queue of children that was very reminiscent of the meal queue in the orphanage. She later got hold of some fence pieces and animals and made a *shamba* [homestead], looking at it long and hard with a very sad expression. A young boy, Daniel, was gathering pieces of railway track and spent a long time running a train back and forth. Chris was also preoccupied with ideas of travel, and he took his Duplo car, complete with driver and passengers, over to our rental car, first running it along the bonnet and then flying his car over ours as if it were an aeroplane. Most striking of all was James, who made a *shamba* very like Mary's, but his was in an upturned frisbee, and he put it on the back of a tricycle before pedalling off, glancing back with a look of absolute triumph. This was a little boy who constantly carried a black headscarf, from which he could not be parted and which was now tied onto his head as he pedalled away carrying his *shamba*.

It quickly became clear that there was a marked difference in the play of children who had had some experience of family life (of parents) and those who had not. Dawn and many of the others had been in the orphanage all their lives. By contrast, Daniel had arrived aged 3 years and had recently met with extended family members who might adopt him. Chris and Mary were also late arrivals, having been left at the orphanage gate after the death of their mothers from Aids. James' mother was also a victim of Aids, and although she had died when James was only a baby, everybody was convinced that the scarf he was so attached to was some kind of a reminder of her.

It was these same children who eventually began to look to us to admire the things they had made. After a while, they lost interest in the toys and began to be actively interested in us, wanting to play games, ask questions, and practise speaking English. The children whose entire lives had been spent living as part of the crowd did not seek out any adult attention or assistance. When we visited the nursery, we could see how this situation would come about. One carer had to look after several babies as well as contribute to the care of the older children. The babies were clean and well fed and lay in comfortable cots but obviously received very little in the way of one-to-one, playful attention. We focused our energies on making contact with a very cut-off, floppy-looking 9-month-old baby, Brian, who at first did not react to our voices or our tentative touch. After about twenty minutes of persistent talking, singing, and gentle touching, he made eye contact and allowed himself to be lifted into a sitting position, watching our movements and responding to the singing of the older girls who had been watching what we had been doing and who were excited about the bag of rattles and cuddly toys we had provided. They began to make friendly overtures to the other babies, and it was heart-rending to have to leave Brian, who quickly slipped back down onto his mattress.

What is the relevance of this observation to formal education in Europe? Even within our own society, it is apparent that children enter school having had very different experiences of play. In nurseries and infant classes, it is recognized that the children will need plenty of opportunity for play, but it is sometimes couched in terms of their not being ready for proper work, rather than in terms of play being a form of developmental work, of real and crucially important learning. Young children who do not know how to play, or whose play is inhibited or impoverished, are a cause for concern, in terms of both their emotional development and their capacity for creative learning.

Inhibitions in play

The following is a brief survey of some of the ways in which inhibitions in play may manifest themselves in the classroom or playground.

Children who cannot play alone

Some children cannot play for any length of time without adult reinforcement. They may be described as lacking concentration, whereas the problem is actually one of not having been helped to separate from their earliest caregiver. These are children who have not been able, for whatever reason, to introject a sustaining parental object. They require the actual parent (or substitute) to be present to facilitate their engagement with the outside world and, without company, will slip into passivity and aimlessness.

Children who only play alone

There are children who never try to join in with others and never seem to seek out the interest or approval of an adult. They may play in parallel with other children without seeming troubled at being left out or different. They are sometimes mistakenly characterized as "independent" or "self-sufficient" whereas it may be more accurate to think of them as children who have not had the kind of experience described above in the observations of Timothy. They have not had the opportunity to play in the presence of a playful, attentive adult, sharing and celebrating their achievements. The lone play may be a desperate attempt to hold themselves together, to hold anxiety at bay. If it is a very entrenched pattern, it may be that any awareness of anxiety is out of reach and that the child is caught up in a phantasy of self-sufficient omnipotence.

Adhesive play

Imitation is an important element of play, but it is a cause for concern if a child's play is purely imitative. Children playing in a "home corner" may happily engage in cooking, ironing, pouring cups of tea, and so on, and the play will seem lively and purposeful. However, careful observation may reveal that some children are trying out identities and developing stories in their minds about the activity, while others are simply repeating sequences with no development and little enjoyment. These same children may arrange furniture and dolls in dolls' houses in an accurate way but never develop a story about the house or its occupants. They may be the children who go on to prefer copying to free drawing and who will have difficulty with creative writing.

A particular version of adhesive play is when there is an over-reliance on characters from TV, films, or books. Most children go through phases when they are passionate about the Telly Tubbies or Thomas the Tank Engine and when they cannot be separated from their Spiderman outfit or their Harry Potter wand. In such a phase, the child will want to collect all the paraphernalia and will reject all other possibilities. If the craze coincides with some external cause of anxiety such as a start at school or the birth of a sibling, it may go on for some considerable time. However, the healthy child will be able to function as himself as well as in character when required to do so and will eventually move on to something new. The discarded character is likely then to be disparaged as "babyish" or may be stowed away in a cupboard as a reminder of earlier times, rather like Timothy's baby-gym.

This kind of identification is a cause for concern when the child becomes totally immersed in a character, when they cannot be distracted from it, and when a demand that they be themselves brings about high anxiety. Children who have difficulty with symbolic thinking may actually believe themselves to be Spiderman or whoever is the chosen alter ego.

Parents and teachers often need help to show a little bit of healthy boredom in the face of repetitive games or identifications that seem to have become stuck and sterile. There is a danger that the adults "buy into" the child's version of the world by using the preferred game or adopted character as part of a reward system. If a child is apparently at his happiest when dressed as Superman, it is hard not to use this as a bargaining chip, thereby reinforcing the idea that it is the most attractive and safest option and that other possibilities are unattractive or frightening.

Concrete play: failures in symbolization

Among the group of children whose play is largely imitative, there may be some who cannot manage symbolic play because of some actual or partial failure in their capacity to differentiate between fantasy and reality. They cannot reliably tell the difference between real and pretend. Traumatized children very often suffer from this kind of confusion. One example was a child patient in psychotherapy who had come close to death with meningitis at age 10 days. When he became frozen in fear at some sudden sound from outside the room, he would try to remain focused on his play but would suddenly expect the animal figures to eat the carpet/grass or would try to climb inside the doll's house as if he were the same size as the dolls. He once tried to stand on a drawing of a ladder and was unable to hear his therapist reminding him that it was a pretend ladder. On other occasions, when calm and confident, he was perfectly clear about the difference between toys and real animals or people.

Another example of this comes from a primary school class-room where a support teacher found herself having to reassure her pupil that the model of a volcano that the class had made together would not actually erupt. He had suddenly frozen in front of it, and when she commented on this, he asked her in a strangled voice whether the lava would reach his estate.

Puzzles and computer games

There are a large number of children who do not actually confuse real and pretend but who are suspicious of fantasy and have a marked preference for reality. These are the children who will prefer factual books to fiction and who may veer towards activities such as jigsaws and computer games. They like certainty and are reassured by knowing that there is a correct solution to a problem. They are also reassured by being able to repeat the same procedures over and over again and always to achieve the same outcome.

This group of children may do very well in most aspects of formal education and are not usually a trouble to their teachers. However, it is worth questioning to what extent their rejection of the more free-floating, creative aspects of play is a defensive turning away from uncertainty and perhaps from the world of relationships. If being asked to join in a different kind of activity causes intolerable anxiety, there may be a need for further exploration of the child's overall development.

Children who cannot share

In every nursery or reception class there will be some children who have had no previous experience of sharing or taking turns. For most, the realization that they are suddenly one of many is painful but manageable, and they soon come to terms with the "rules" of the classroom. They will turn towards their peers, seeing new opportunities for friendships and shared games. For others, the reality of being expected to wait or to share is more than they can tolerate. Some turn away in a sulky or despairing way, whereas others compete for every ounce of adult attention, every toy, and every privilege. Among the latter group will be some who seem entirely ruthless in their disregard for other children. They may be physically aggressive towards a child they perceive as a threat, or they may employ cunning to make sure that they get the most popular toy, the first turn, and so on. The other children in the class become hated "siblings" who have to be put in their place, representing, as they do, the babies who have ousted them from their privileged place with Mummy.

How easily this conflict will get resolved will depend to a large degree on how the adults at home and at school address it. It will also depend on the disposition of the child himself. Some children are simply more envious and unforgiving than others and need a great deal of help in coming to terms with "the facts of life", as presented in Hamish Canham's opening chapter (chapter 1).

Symbolic play, re-enactment, and "working through"

In imaginative, symbolic play, ideas emerge and storylines de-velop. They often involve passionate feelings, and there may be hatred and violence as well as shocking imagery such as monsters, blood, and poison. Children's play often involves police cars and ambulances, hospitals, death, and childbirth. It is sometimes a dif-ficult task to tease out what derives from actual experience and what is imaginative, to tell the difference between re-enactment and symbolic play. This is a serious issue in cases where judge-ments have to be made as to whether or not children are enacting something that has happened to them or that they have witnessed. In child-protection cases, there is a strong temptation to look for evidence from children's play in the form of re-enactment. If a child accurately simulates sexual intercourse in play, it can make everyone feel more confident about concluding that sexual abuse has occurred, or at least that the child has been exposed to inap-propriate sexual activity.

Children do sometimes re-enact events in a way that is utterly convincing, particularly events involving violence between adults or sexual activity. Teachers and others may be left not knowing whether there is violence at home or whether the child has been watching soap opera. Whichever is the case, there is still a question as to why the child is incorporating the scenes into his play, why he is showing you, and what the meaning of it might be for him. All kinds of anxieties and conflicts are worked through in play. Oedipal concerns and ideas about separation, loss, and sibling rivalry (real or imagined siblings) get acted out and rendered less frightening in the process. Children try out all kinds of identifications—playing the role of mother, father, baby, policeman, doctor, super-hero, and many more. Most children are very aware that they are playing and manage to regulate their emotional engagement with the drama. Only if the feelings become too intense or convincing do children need to extricate themselves and check back with the real world in the shape of parent, nursery worker, or teacher. In this sense, play acts as a bridge between the conscious and unconscious realms of experience, between the external and internal worlds of the developing child.

Summary

There is a major role for teachers in fostering play and in promoting a playful approach to learning. If work can be established as something enjoyable in the early stages of formal education, the two activities are less likely to become so polarized in later years.

Children's play can be very misleading, and the key to reaching some understanding of what is going on is in the kind of observation that is described in chapter 7. By observing a child's play over time and in a variety of contexts, and by examining both the content of the play and the impact on the observer, it may be possible to reach some conclusion as to the internal-world experience of the child. This kind of observation would, in my view, inform classroom practice as well as any individual educational or therapeutic intervention.

CHAPTER FOUR

Latency

Hamish Canham

I shall start by giving a general overview of this period of child development, with some ideas from psychoanalytic theory about what is going on for children in the so-called latency period—that is, between about 5 and 12 years of age. It is impossible to be precise about years, but I shall divide the period into three phases, starting with younger children, 5- to 7-year-olds; then the middle age group of 7-, 8-, and 9-year-olds; and, lastly, the older latency children who are approaching puberty and adolescence.

Before looking in more detail at what latency means as a developmental phase, it would be helpful to paint a picture of typical latency children. The images that come immediately to my mind are as follows:

> *I think of them as wearing school uniforms, being relatively polite and respectful, going out to play, and doing things like football for boys, French skipping for girls, ball games against the wall, clapping games, clubs and secret societies, crazes like yo-yos, conkers, and hopscotch, and lots of collecting and swapping of stamps, marbles, etc. They go to "cubs" or "brownies" and take great pride in getting badges.*

47

This list is a personal one and clearly somewhat specific to a particular time and place. Everyone will have a different version depending on their memories of their own childhood and on children they have subsequently known. However, an up-to-date list might not be so very different. There would still be football and probably some of the traditional playground games such as skipping and chase. Collections might be of Pokemon cards, Harry Potter badges, or football stickers, but these would be traded and swapped in much the same way as before.

This tendency to collect is now well understood and exploited commercially, with vast arrays of merchandise following any new film or TV series. Themed stationery, toys, and clothing are widely advertised and made available in all newsagents and supermarkets. It is matter for debate as to whether commercial pressure can actually change the nature of the child's experience of latency, dictating the direction it takes and the moment at which it gives way to adolescence.

Latency: an overview

Latency is the period in a child's life which is sandwiched between two rather tempestuous times: babyhood preceding it and adolescence beckoning. It is a stage that is characterized by relative emotional tranquillity. It is because of the calmness characteristic of this period that it is referred to as latency. Freud wrote about this period in *Three Essays on the Theory of Sexuality* (1905d) as being when "sexuality normally advances no further". It is a period of repression of instincts (not just sexual ones but aggressive ones too) and organization of defences, which gives the child a degree of stability. Interestingly, such is the power of repression in this period that many people find it hard to recall the detail of these years in later life.

Melanie Klein expanded Freud's ideas on latency. She held that latency was a period of life where the apparent stability was not just because the child's sexuality and other instincts were repressed, but because they were split off and played out in games such as cowboys and Indians or heroes and villains, or tightly controlled in rather obsessional activity such as collecting and cataloguing collections. According to Mrs Klein, it is by these means that internal conflict gets played out in the external world during latency. Energy that was previously employed in curiosity about the mother's body, and in what was happening in parental sexuality, is diverted into curiosity about the outside world. Erik Erikson (1950) called the latency period the "era of industry" when children settle down to learning and amassing informa-tion. Latency children often have encyclopaedic knowledge of one topic, whether it is dinosaurs or football teams. All this de-fensiveness does, of course, have its advantages. It allows for a period of undisturbed learning at school, as well as adaptation in the family. There is a sense in which some areas of development need to be held in abeyance so that other areas can grow, but the disadvantage may be that there is a constriction of emotionality and creativity

The space in between the family and the social world is vitally important at this age. It is why the theme of separation and reun-ion with family is so central to much of children's literature. This whole area is explored in Margaret and Michael Rustin's book on children's fiction, *Narratives of Love and Loss* (1987). There is the strange in-between land of Narnia in C. S. Lewis' books, and innu-merable children's adventure stories take place in boarding schools or on holiday, away from adults. Arthur Ransome's "Swallows and Amazons" novels, for example, bring to life a world of long summer holidays with few of the usual routines and restrictions. More recently, the *Home Alone* films have explored the capacities of children to fend for themselves without the protection, or interfer-ence, of adults.

Latency children tend to go around in small groups, and issues are very clear-cut for them. They divide up quickly into cliques or groups based on gender, age, or neighbourhood or on particular hobbies or activities. In this way, difficult issues of good and bad are regulated and painful feelings are dealt with by putting them into others, into "them".

I would like to illustrate this particular theme with a descrip-tion of a therapy group for children between the ages of 5 and 12 years. This material illustrates how this particular tendency to form into groups can so easily spill over into bullying. There were six children in the group.

This is a quote from my session notes:

> The other children are playing at the sink. It seems very cosy, when Vicky comes along to join in; Sandra, who has herself been ostracized at school, says nastily, "go away, Vicky". My co-therapist and I stop the play and talk about how it might look as if they are playing a nice game together, but it is only nice for them if someone else is left out. They find it hard to listen. George turns on the tap so that hot water gushes over a crocodile in a cage. We say to him that this treatment of the crocodile is similar to what we have been saying—that one person is being treated cruelly.

What is going on in this group also illustrates the importance of play for children in latency as a means by which they can external-ize and explore conflict. In play, children can explore aspects both of themselves and of other people. One might say that through the crocodile in the cage, George is exploring both what it is to be the persecutor—when he turns on the hot tap—and, through identi-fication, what it is like to be on the receiving end of persecution. George's exploration, through symbolic play, contains his experi-ence in a way that is very different from the interchange between Sandra and Vicky.

In spite of the apparent calm on the surface, latency children work hard to keep anxiety at bay and often show their primitive fears in a preoccupation with monsters, dragons, witches, and wicked stepmothers. Night-time fears include ideas about what might be under the bed, behind the curtain, coming in through the window. In the daytime, in the safety of their homogeneous group, the healthy latency child has space for exploring the world and will learn with ease. However, it is likely to be the kind of learning that focuses on facts and figures and on the mastery of skills. Learning in early childhood and in adolescence is a much more uncertain matter, with peaks and troughs and much more anxiety.

Early latency

What brings a child of about 5 years to the point where he can settle down for a bit? A baby or toddler has had a period of time to find out about his parents. For a small child, the idea of what mother or father is like can seem to oscillate wildly and depends very much on the baby or toddler's internal state, as well as on what the parent is like in reality. By about 5 years of age, the child should have had sufficient experience of matching his internal picture of his parents against reality, and hopefully he will have inside himself a more secure mental representation of his parents—what one could call a good internal parent or parental object.

In conjunction with this development taking place in the child's internal world, certain things happen in a child's external life which he needs to find ways of dealing with. At age 5, children in this country go to school. It may be that the loss of their mother's exclusive or near-exclusive attention has happened at an earlier age, or over a prolonged period of time, but there is a definite punctuation point at 5 years of age. It is then that involvement with mother and family becomes less important and the focus moves to school—to teacher and peer group. While family relationships remain central to children's sense of security, they begin to explore further afield. This is the beginning of feelings of independence and real agency, as opposed to the phantasied omnipotence of earlier childhood.

I think that this is why birthdays are so often tinged with sadness, because they are not just a celebration of what is to come, or the point that has been reached, but also a mourning for what has passed.

A 4-year-old patient of mine was just coming up to his fifth birthday. In his session, he pretends he is in his classroom. First he pretends he is the teacher. Then he pretends he is in a race against his classmates. He seems rather worried, and I say that I think he is scared of being left behind and that others will win the race. The boy says, "yes, I am", and goes on to tell me that it will be his birthday in a few days' time. I say that I think what he is worried about is growing up and being a 5-year-old boy. At this he flops down across the table in the middle of the room and says, "How do you play football?" This little boy associated being 5 with knowing the rules of "big boys' games" and felt rather unequal to the task.

Going to school confronts all children with different rules from family life. At school they are expected not just to know how to play football, but to cooperate with other children and to do a range of things for themselves. Where the difference between home and school is, perhaps, most noticed is at mealtimes. The intimacy between a child and mother to do with feeding and toileting is still very strong at age 5. It is very common for children first at school to find school dinners too strange to eat or to be unable to go to the toilet. They have to get used to the different food and to be being served in a much more impersonal way.

Going to school also means that a child has to integrate the two worlds. This can often be very hard. Teachers are often called "Mummy" by mistake, and 5-year-olds develop passionate feelings about their teachers and feel their loyalty split between home and school. It is also a hard time for parents, who, having been used to being the main figures in their child's life, find it upsetting when every sentence is prefaced with "my teacher says . . .". Most 5-year-olds are beginning to focus on friendships, but for many the teacher remains the main focal point for some time. At age 5, girls and boys still play together. They do not yet have the skills necessary for negotiation, and there is a lot of falling-out and making-up, with best friends becoming worst enemies for very little reason.

At age 5, children's play will tend to be to do with "mothers and fathers" and "school", reflecting the preoccupation at this stage with growing up and with relationships. At the same time, there is the beginning of discovering the peer group, and children will come home with words and expressions that begin to mark separateness from the family. A 6-year-old girl, for example, suddenly greeted every request from her mother with "Whatever", spoken with a studied air of weary indifference.

This early latency age also marks the beginning of learning to read and write, but there is still a tendency for 5-, 6-, and 7-year-olds to think in a rather concrete way. A child of this age who has lost his mother in a shop, for example, may go into a complete panic in the belief that she has really disappeared. This is because an internal representation of mother is not yet fully developed. Many children, of course, rely on concrete reminders of parents and home, like blankets or teddy bears. Children in early latency often feel their parents to be all-knowing and invincible. Unlike adolescents—and, indeed, toddlers—they tend not to challenge their parents, because just for now they want the security that goes with having the "perfect" parents. This, then, is a period of transition from babyhood to childhood.

Middle latency

In middle latency, the child leaves the relative security of the infant school (Years One and Two) and has to move to junior school. This is what one might call the "Blue Peter" era of childhood, when children make collections and construct things out of "sticky-back plastic" and loo rolls. They develop enthusiasms for particular causes, often connected with animal welfare, and they join clubs and societies which have their own rules and rituals. Routine and regularity are a very important part of middle latency. Whereas young children seem very interested in parents as a couple and what they are up to, children of this age seem to push sex and sexuality to the backs of their minds. If reference is made to sex, as it might be in the playground, it tends to be in a denigrating or smutty way, not at all linked with wanting to think about sex as being to do with love or for procreation.

The same group of children I described earlier give us a glimpse of a mid-latency view of parental sexuality:

> Linda and Sandra dress up as a pirate (Linda), and his gal (Sandra). Linda tells Sandra to "come to bed" and, lunging at her chest, demands "where are your tits?" Sandra is coyly led to the makeshift bed in the Wendy house, but as they lie down she says to Linda—"well, aren't you going to take out your teeth?"

This is a parodied view of parental sexuality—as something rather vulgar and with the parents getting "past it".

One way of looking at this age group is as a time when earlier discoveries are reinforced. One of the most important discoveries is who you are. Before he can explore all the different aspects of his character, as happens in adolescence, a child needs to feel safely grounded in his identity. It is for this reason perhaps that boys and girls tend to separate during these mid-latency years. They do not want their sexuality challenged. It is only once a child feels safe as a boy or a girl that he or she can think what it is like to be someone else. It is at this period of development that children typically want to follow gendered role models, with boys having ideas of becoming soldiers, footballers, or policemen and girls thinking in terms of becoming nurses or models. This stereotypical view is rarely challenged at this age in spite of the reality of everyone knowing about female police officers or male models.

School is the place where children can find the security of sameness. However, it is also the place where differences begin to show up. Children with difficulties come to the attention of teachers. When the normal pattern of development goes askew and healthy defences have not been established, there is no period of calm and life becomes increasingly turbulent.

Latency children are not without aggression, but on the whole it is externalized in competitive games and sports. It seems that games are a way of keeping competitiveness out of family relationships. Winning board games, being chosen for sports teams, or accumulating gold stars or stickers become all-important. Middle latency is also the time when children amass huge collections of things, and if a group of friends all collect similar things, it binds them together in a tight unit where rivalries over who has collected what can be played out safely. Children can learn to compare, barter, and swap. They can feel rich, either because of their possessions or their accumulated specialist knowledge.

Late latency

As a child approaches 10, 11, or 12 years of age, he faces the end of latency and the onset of adolescence. Late latency is again a kind of in-between stage—no longer firmly rooted in the middle of childhood but not yet in adolescence. This is perhaps the most unpredictable stage, since puberty propels children into adolescence at different ages. There will also be a wide variation in physical maturity between boys and girls, with boys lagging at least a year or two behind. The dilemma facing children on the cusp of adolescence was illustrated to me by a 12-year-old girl patient who was beginning to mature physically. At one level she quite enjoyed the beginnings of teenage life, but at another level she was really very scared about it. She drew a picture of herself as an angel, but the picture stopped at the waist. I thought she was desperately trying to keep herself in latency and to deny her sexual maturity. Puberty tends to be easier for boys than for girls as the physical changes are fewer and occur later. In fact, if a boy does have early pubertal development, he is likely to enjoy high status among his peers.

At home it is at this age that children begin to want to be different from their parents and may even be slightly embarrassed by them. They may be less willing to accept adult guidance and discipline. They want to choose what they wear, what they eat, what time they go to bed and get up. The problem for parents, teachers, and others working with children of this age is how to foster growing independence and yet continue to provide a secure framework for living.

Relationships to adults at this age become complicated by growing sexual awareness. Boys may want to move away from their mothers; they may feel small if they are too close to mothers at a time when they want to feel big and masculine. Boys may want to grow closer to their fathers, but there may also be some rivalry which fathers can find hard to manage. Girls in late latency may want to identify with their mothers, imagining they can become "sisters" or "best friends", suddenly hanging around on the fringes of their mother's social group. Girls will look to their fathers or other grown-up men to see how they are responding to their new sexuality. This is sometimes a tricky time for male teachers and may be so for fathers who are unprepared for this new development.

At school, what is noticeable if development is proceeding along healthy tracks is that children's way of thinking begins to change. It shifts from the rather concrete focus on matters of fact into the territory of abstract ideas. Children begin to have opinions about issues and to use their minds to develop an argument. They may be moved by nature, by poetry, or by art without really understanding why, and the focus of their altruistic concern is likely to shift from the animal world to human issues of poverty, war, and injustice.

Failures of latency

There are a large number of children in schools who do not achieve this latency state of mind, children whose real-life experiences clamour for attention in ways that cannot be ignored. These cannot wait, and they intrude relentlessly into every facet of a child's life. These children carry around such painful undigested feelings that they cannot achieve the state of mind necessary for concentrating in class, doing homework, having friendships, and so on. Some children, as we know, cannot even sit down, listen, keep quiet, or relax sufficiently to go to sleep.

CASE EXAMPLE

An 8-year-old boy, Peter, was referred to the clinic after his parents' marriage broke up in particularly acrimonious circumstances. He witnessed a lot of arguing between his parents, and he was aware of his father's infidelities. His father eventually left home. Prior to the marriage break-up, Peter had been well-behaved at school and at home, but he suddenly became very violent, threatening to stab his mother with a knife, wanting to kill her. He also threatened to jump out of a window himself.

At the beginning of his therapy, he drew many pictures of volcanoes erupting and of cannons firing. These volcanoes seemed to me to be Peter's picture of how his calm latency world had been exploded by his parent's marital difficulties, leaving him full of rage at what had happened and unable to keep his anger from erupting. I think he also felt the core of his world was shaken, as he could no longer trust adults to be reliable. His picture of me was represented by the cannons. I was not a helpful Mr Canham but a Mr Cannon, likely to drop a bombshell on him at any time or fire him into a world for which he was not yet ready. His development was very disrupted, and he was left feeling unsettled at a time when his peers were mainly calm, and this led to all sorts of difficulties in his friendships.

Sadly, many of the children we are likely to encounter in our work have probably not experienced the calmness of this period of childhood. Peter's experience of family breakdown is far from unusual, and I could compile a long list of external-world events that have an intrusive and damaging effect on the latency child's development. High on the list must be experiences of sexual and physical abuse, abandonment, trauma, and dislocation. These extreme experiences simply do not allow for any period of calm. Many children are propelled from babyhood straight into a kind of adolescence or even adulthood with no period where the sorting-out of the kind of feelings and anxieties I have described has happened. School can sometimes play a vital role in providing the most traumatized children with a safe place where predictable routines and consistent adult concern can go some way to facilitating an experience of latency.

I would want to make an argument for protecting the period of relative calm that children need from untimely intrusions, such as premature exposure to violence and sex on the TV and elsewhere. If "adult" issues intrude into the world of the latency child, it becomes difficult, if not impossible, for him to employ the defences needed to keep this kind of thing out of immediate consciousness. It could be argued, too, that the world of commerce, with the collusion of the media, is actively propelling latency-aged children into adolescence through an emphasis on appearance and on the desirability of "young teens'" fashion, pop idols, and so on.

A latency state of mind

Judith Edwards (1999) makes the point that latency is not so much a phase as an achievement, a state of being that is a necessary feature of childhood and one that we return to at times throughout the life cycle.

A latency state of mind is one we all need to go back into from time to time. Anne Alvarez (1989) writes about this as being able to develop "a certain sort of object-relation with one's own thoughts". Concentration on a thought, a task, or a subject requires focusing of attention but also the capacity to ignore other thoughts and feelings. She stresses, therefore, how the splitting that is so characteristic of latency has an important developmental function, which is by no means purely defensive and which remains a feature of our psychic repertoire throughout life.

CHAPTER FIVE

Adolescence

In the following extract from her autobiographical novel, *Anita and Me* (1996), Meera Syal describes something of the nature of early adolescence in the 1950s. Meena, the troubled and rebellious 10-year-old daughter of first-generation immigrants from India, follows every move of her idol—the loud-mouthed and streetwise Anita.

Early in the novel, Meena declared, "I was happy to follow her a few paces behind, knowing that I was privileged to be in her company." Later, when she had caught Anita's attention by taking part in a number of acts of antisocial, minor delinquency, Meena described the way they spent their days:

> We did nothing special, beyond strolling round the park with carefully cultivated bored expressions, exploring the abandoned pigsties (secret play dens of her latency years) with adult disdain, shimmying down to Mr Ormerod's corner shop with unimpressed faces, always aware that we were simply too big and beautiful for Tollington and making sure that everyone else knew it as well. [pp. 133–134]
>
> Anita and I would leaf through the current issue of *Jackie*, doing the quizzes on each other, "How Do You Know If He

Fancies You?" planning our wardrobes and interior décor for the flat in London we would buy together when we reached eighteen . . .

When I say that we talked, what I mean is that Anita talked and I listened with the appropriate appreciative noises. But I never had to force my admiration, it flowed from every pore because Anita made me laugh like nobody else; she gave voice to all the wicked things I had often thought but kept zipped up inside my good girl's winter coat. Her irreverence was high summer for me. . . . I would gasp for air and wait for the next revelation, each one tilting my small world slightly off its axis so I saw the familiar and the mundane through new, cynical eyes, Anita's eyes. [p. 138]

Meena had been catapulted into early adolescence—or, rather, into pseudo-adolescence—by her mother's pregnancy. An only child for her first ten years, Meena had avoided recognition of her parent's sexual relationship and when Sunil arrived could not bear to think about this product of her parent's intercourse and then to have to witness the closeness of her brother's feeding relationship with *her* mother. Her father was hurt that she simultaneously turned away from him ("I do talk to you. But I've got me mates now, haven't I? I'm dead busy, me.") and also became vociferous in her rejection of their Indian friends, the Punjabi language, clothes, food, and culture. Her parents might have come from India, but *she* was English.

As is typical of adolescence, the splitting was extreme, and she embraced all things English without discrimination. Her desire to belong to what she saw as the most exciting group became all that mattered. ("We both agreed there was no point putting so much energy into posturing and looking mean if you didn't have some others around to applaud or take the blame when things turned nasty.") Anita was all that her family was not—brash, rude, dishonest, and English—and Meena saw her as her "passport to acceptance".

She succeeded in manoeuvring herself onto the edges of adolescent life, but we go on to read about the gradual disillusionment of the younger girl as she first feels betrayed when Anita gets a boyfriend and is then further disturbed by the spread of racism ("Paki-bashing") among those she considered to be her friends.

With her grandmother's arrival from India came a shift in the family dynamic, and Meena found a new position for herself, more comfortably in a transitional place, moving back and forth between latency and adolescence. In this position, she was able to "forgive" her young brother for existing and even to try out an identification with her mother as caregiver.

Meera Syal's account highlights many of the central features of adolescence: a reawakening of awareness of parental sexuality, a turning away from family culture towards something very different, the beginnings of an interest in the opposite gender, a rejection of concern for educational achievement, and a flirtation with life outside the confines of the law. This autobiographical novel moves on to describe the way in which some of these conflicts get resolved, or at least are brought back into perspective, in time for Meena to do herself justice in the eleven-plus examination.

As with all stages of personality development, adolescence does not start or finish at a particular age, nor does it last for a particular length of time. Indeed, it is only fairly recently that it has been recognized as a phenomenon and has featured so centrally in literature and in daily discourse. Debate goes on as to whether it is a universally recognizable phase of development and what might be the cultural determinates of adolescent experience. Some of the detail in the description of Meena's adolescence belongs specifically to the 1950s and 1960s and will resonate in a particular way with those of us who grew up in that era. Other aspects of the description will be familiar to all. This is because adolescents have certain developmental tasks in common, but the context, in Western societies, varies according to popular culture. Indeed, it is the specific role of adolescents to drive popular culture forward to whatever is to be its next manifestation.

Lanyado (Lanyado & Horne, 1999) suggests that it is possible to identify certain "universal emotional leitmotifs" which she sees as operating "independently of historical period, culture or patterns of parenting and child rearing". For psychoanalytic theorists, these leitmotifs would be the emotional tasks involved in moving from latency, when curiosity about oneself and about sexual relationships is put on hold, to adulthood, where the expectation is that one knows oneself, has separated to a large extent from family, has established ways of making relationships, and is able to tolerate uncertainty and ambivalence. The adolescent is seen as subject to a massive resurgence of curiosity, a renewed preoccupation with oedipal conflict, and a constantly changing set of interests and allegiances. Splitting again predominates, with the accompanying reliance on idealization and denigration. The need to belong leads teenagers to come together in homogeneous groups, sharing interests, clothing, language. The need to exclude others leads groups to behave as gangs, projecting all the unwanted aspects of their personalities into other groups, who are ridiculed and sometimes actively attacked. The lines along which these divisions occur are all too readily those of race, social class, or gender. The psychic changes happen alongside the physical changes, and the interrelationship between the growth of the personality and physical development becomes more and more complex as hormones affect moods and behaviour and as the changing physical body preoccupies the mind of the growing individual.

The tasks laid out for the adolescent in psychoanalytic theory point to a degree of psychic struggle and pain. Coming to terms with one's parents' sexuality, with one's own strengths and weaknesses, and with the need to make choices about how one spends one's life involves pain. It is easy, then, to underplay the excitement, energy, and creativity that are also a part of adolescent life. One argument might be that the adult world emphasizes the pain of the process in order to defend itself against the envy that is provoked by seeing young people flexing their intellectual, social, and sexual muscles.

Western, media-dominated, popular culture presents adolescence as a carefree time, when life is there to be enjoyed and anything is possible. Teenagers are encouraged to grasp opportunities and experiment with ideas and activities, to have a good time before they have to take on the heavy burdens of responsibility that are seen as coming with work, long-term relationships, and parenthood. The popular press simultaneously requires of the adolescent a degree of self-restraint. The young person is expected to "play the field" but not to put him/herself at risk of sexually transmitted diseases. Nobody should become unintentionally pregnant, and homosexual young people should wait until they are 18, or at least should keep their activity secret. Getting drunk is to be expected, but it should not lead to unruly, violent, or criminal behaviour. Teenagers are expected to resist an ever-proliferating array of drugs, or at least to restrict themselves to a moderate intake and to know when to stop.

Adolescence and education

The purpose of this chapter is to look at the relationship between education and adolescence, from the point of view of how the adolescent meets the challenge of formal education but also from the opposite perspective: how does the teacher, the school, and the college adapt itself to cope with the challenge of educating large numbers of individuals in this phase of development?

Just at the point when the developing individual is at his most labile, he is expected to impose a considerable degree of self-regulation on his behaviour. Alex Coren (1997) makes a similar point in relation to education:

> The demand to be educated during adolescence confronts us with what appears to be a paradox: at a time of life when we most want to forget, act impulsively, or avoid reflection, we most need to remember, comply and perform. We accept that adolescence is a period of rebelliousness, confusion and upheaval; yet at the same time expect our adolescents to engage in what we call "formal education" which makes demands on them that . . . are difficult to meet. [p. 5]

This is not to suggest that a free-flowing laissez-faire approach is what is required. Margot Waddell (course lecture) argues that the routine requirements of school and family life need to be firmly in place to provide the developing adolescent with a structure in what might otherwise be too formless a way of life. She suggests that, without this, the adolescent is left in a very frightening position, believing his internal turmoil to be uncontained and uncontainable. As Coren puts it, "Rebelling against something is infinitely safer than rebelling against nothing." Appeasement leads to contempt and to the unconscious fear of retaliation that inevitably accompanies feelings of omnipotence.

Secondary transfer

In the United Kingdom, secondary transfer takes place for most children at the age of 11 years. This does not necessarily coincide neatly with puberty and the onset of adolescence. Indeed, the introduction of middle schools by some authorities in the late twentieth century might have been seen to be an attempt to provide age-appropriate education for a range of pupils in transition from latency to adolescence. Puberty is happening earlier than hitherto, particularly in girls, and many Year Six groups are beginning to have a distinctly adolescent feel to them. However, Year Seven and Eight classes in secondary schools will still have a significant number of children who have not yet reached puberty, who cling together for safety, or who hang around on the edges of much of what goes on, like anxious spectators. On moving to secondary school, children have to face the fact that they are once again at the bottom of the heap. Having enjoyed a privileged position in primary school, as the oldest and most "knowing" group, they are suddenly pitched into a new system where they know very little. Even those who were ready to leave the primary school and who had outgrown its latency-oriented environment have to come to terms with the loss of something safe and familiar. As Coren suggests, they have two new sets of rules to learn. They have to learn how to conform to the demands of the secondary education system at the same time as learning the "rules" of adolescence—which are all about not conforming.

At the point of entry into secondary school, most pupils do not know the building, the teachers, or the routines. They may know very few, if any, of their peers. The timetable is baffling, they get lost, they take the wrong books to the wrong lesson, they are fearful of being bullied, and they worry about drawing the wrong kind of attention to themselves. They may also be filled with excitement and satisfaction at having achieved this significant milestone. They may wear their new uniform with pride, only slowly realizing that the "proper" thing to do as a true adolescent is to wear as little of it as possible or to wear it with a proper degree of disdain. A recent television documentary about a group of children starting secondary school showed an 11-year-old girl preparing for her first day. She and her friends had agreed on how they would do their hair and had bought identical school bags. This girl was clearly not yet pubertal but was talking with bravado about which boys she might fancy. On the first morning, her mother expressed anxiety, but the child herself was very calm. She insisted that her mother should not accompany her beyond the school gate. It would not create the right image. There was then a very touching sequence, with the girl setting off and then returning to say goodbye a second time, very much like a toddler returning to a secure base for reassurance. Her mother was offering to go with her, and she eventually said "if you want to", while looking around anxiously to see who might be witnessing the scene. Her mother went with her some of the way, until she plucked up the courage to rush ahead and into school. This seemed to sum up so much of a young adolescent's task: how to move away from home and family in manageable stages.

Secondary schools have to find ways to cope with an intake of pupils who are at different stages in their physical development and at different stages in their progress towards independence. Schools tend to have two responses. First, they impress upon the newcomers that this is *secondary* school and that they will be expected to work hard and to develop the capacity for independent study. At the same time, they are given a very clear message as to who is in charge, who makes the rules, and how they will be enforced. It is as if the teachers are determined to establish a system, knowing that it will all too quickly be buffeted by adolescent rebellion. All kinds of sanctions are put in place in an attempt to hold the boundaries and maintain a framework for teaching and learning which will see the young people through to school-leaving age or transfer to higher education. This mirrors in a very real way the dilemma facing parents of adolescent children. How do parents strike a balance between promoting their children's development by giving them more freedom and yet still impose their authority when necessary?

Adolescents, parents, and schools

It is worth dwelling on the parallel experiences of the family and the school in the face of adolescent development. Parents often comment that having adolescent children is like having infants or toddlers to look after all over again. They are subject to extreme mood swings and are very difficult to please. They are preoccupied with justice and yet never accept responsibility or blame for their own actions. They challenge their external parents and simultaneously seem to lose touch with internal parental figures that might hold them steady. What is not so often recognized is that the parental couple may themselves be destabilized by their children reaching puberty. It shifts their own lives into the next phase, whether they feel ready for it or not. They may be put in touch with unresolved aspects of their own adolescence or catapulted forward to having to imagine grandparenthood or life as a couple without children to care for. Their child's oedipal preoccupations take on a different hue when sexual activity is a real possibility, and parents find that confrontations become charged with currents of sexuality, aggression, and violence. Fathers feel that their authority (and sexual potency) is challenged by sexually mature sons, and mothers feel thrown by their daughter's potential for child bearing. Splitting and projection are an essential part of the adolescent's psychic developmental process, and wedges may be driven between father and mother, acted out by one or other becoming overprotective, over-controlling, or hypercritical.

Exactly the same dynamic is evident in schools, where teachers feel challenged by the developing minds and bodies of their adolescent pupils. In the best of circumstances they may recognize the splitting for what it is, but it is hard to remain steady in the face of a constant barrage of projection. The adolescent's hatred of weakness or impotence may be projected into the teacher who can all too easily lose touch with her own competence in exactly the same way as a parent. Schools as institutions sometimes behave like families, overreacting to the challenges presented and losing touch with any confidence in the solidity of the organization.

The function of the family is to protect and care for children, to support their development, and to facilitate in stages their departure from the family into the outside world. In adolescence the young person's family plays a part in helping him to take important steps in the individuation and separation process. Schools take over some aspects of this role and, as the children reach adolescence, have a duty to help them look out beyond the confines of the education system. Just as some families have difficulty in facilitating their children's separation, some schools do little to support their pupils in developing their independent minds.

Family constellation

The last fifty years has seen a phenomenal increase in the number of lone-parent families. The vast majority of these are single women with children. Of these, some have been left to look after families and some have actively chosen to parent their children alone. There has been an increase in separation and divorce and an increase in reconstituted families: family units coming together in complicated combinations, maintaining complicated relationships with former partners.

A later chapter (chapter 11) looks at the issues for these families in more detail, but it should be noted here that complex family structures can give an adolescent a great deal of work to do in trying to make sense of the adult world and of his potential place within it. Clearly, a lone parent, of either gender, can create the kind of reflective space referred to in relation to the roots of learning in infancy (chapters 1 and 2). If the lone parent's internal objects are robust and sustaining, they can and do fulfil both a maternal and paternal function. However, many lone parents would comment that parenting adolescents has tested their resilience and has led them to lean more than ever on the support of extended family and friends. There may be particular difficulty for adolescents who lose a parent, whether through relationship breakdown or death. For an oedipal adolescent boy, the loss of a father can feel like a horrible realization of his unconscious wish. Similarly, the arrival of a new "father" in a home where the son has held sway with his single mother may both destabilize him and put the new relationship at risk.

Young adolescence

In early adolescence, expressions of rebellion are usually relatively minor. Young teenagers begin to question and reject the way their parents live and to look elsewhere for role models. Although claiming that they are striking out for independence, what they actually do is attach themselves as quickly as possible to a group and adopt its norms. This means accepting the group's preferences in terms of clothing, music, politics, and so forth. Within the safe confines of the group, individuals try out a range of identities, project aspects of themselves into other group members, and gradually learn more about themselves. The sameness of the group enables its members to experiment very carefully with ideas about minor differences. However, real, significant differences cannot be tolerated, and the group is unlikely to be stable for any length of time. Members of the group will become disillusioned, will be seduced by other groups, will be expelled, and, as time moves on, will split off in pairs. Adolescents change their group allegiances with remarkable rapidity, and they expend a huge amount of emotional energy in the process.

School is an important arena for this intense social experimentation, and it can sometimes seem that there is very little time or energy left for the business of getting an education. The extent to which students will be able to learn in these circumstances will depend on many factors. First, it will depend on the extent to which they can keep in touch with their own and their parents' ambitions for the future and how much they fall prey to the adolescent tendency to live for the moment. It will depend on their experience of learning in early childhood and in latency and on whether they have retained an interest in the world beyond their immediate orbit. It will also depend on the curriculum and on their teachers' capacity to be in touch with their preoccupations, tolerant of their excesses, and clear in their expectations.

CHAPTER SIX

Beginnings, endings, and times of transition

This chapter seeks to trace some of the major rites of passage that occur between arrival in nursery or reception class and leaving school to join higher education or the world of work. It looks at parallels between these major points of transition and the routine changes in activity that characterize the school day, the school week, and the academic year.

An enhanced understanding of the significance of beginnings and endings has always been a key aim of applied psychoanalytic thinking. It is crucial not only to the better understanding of each individual child's response to change, but also in thinking about "whole-school policies". Ways of managing new arrivals in school, of structuring the beginning and end of days, of planning for the end of term, preparing children for teacher absence, and so on depend on the degree to which the school recognizes that change provokes anxiety. The task of managing the feelings that accompany beginnings and endings in school life is one that builds on early infantile experience of separations and change. Again it is the school that takes over much of the responsibility for this aspect of development

Clinical vignettes

Emma was 3½ years old when she was referred to the clinic because she would not go to nursery. Indeed, she would not go anywhere outside the home. She would not allow anybody other than her parents to look after her. She would not go into the garden alone and was becoming very frightened of flying insects, of dogs, and of strangers. Her parents described Emma as super-intelligent and spoke with pride about her computer skills. They were convinced that she was more interested in her computer than in people, because everyone they knew was less intelligent than she was. When it was suggested, very gently, that she might actually be frightened of separation from her parents, and from her computer, her mother protested: "How could she be frightened of separation, she has *never* been left alone, not for one moment!"

Thomas, another 3-year-old, was brought to the clinic when his parents became concerned that his development seemed to have got stuck, particularly his speech. His vocabulary was very limited, and he spoke only in baby talk. He would not give up his bottle. In discussion, it emerged that his parents had tried to smooth his way in life so that he had no anxiety. Like Emma, Thomas had not had to manage ordinary frustration. He was overfed: there was to be no waiting, no frustration. At the end of our sessions at the clinic, the room was littered with sticky biscuits—sucked but not eaten. This was a child who had never really experienced hunger. If his mother had to leave him she would sneak away while he was not looking, and his parents would only go out at night after he had fallen asleep. If he awoke they would be summoned home by mobile phone so that he never knew they had been away. It might be said that he had no need of language: his every need was anticipated and dealt with before he could become conscious of it.

These two clinical examples serve as illustrations of difficulties that arose because of a reluctance to face separation, a reluctance to make the transition from one phase of life to the next. Both Thomas and Emma were refusing, in their own ways, to take the next step and were not being helped to do so. Emma's parents did not want to hear what was being said, and we failed to manage our intervention in a way that might have helped them to stop and think. We were much too quick to force a separation onto them, albeit only within the confines of the clinic. They could not bear it and cancelled the next appointment. Thomas's parents, on the other hand, felt that what we said about fear of change made sense, and they began to think differently about their child's needs.

Separation, loss, and change may be painful but are absolutely essential experiences that link with growth, development, and internal strength. In infancy and early childhood, the developing individual has to undergo thousands and thousands of small beginnings and endings, in order to become equipped to deal with later losses and transitions. Every ending, however minor, involves a loss of some kind. Every beginning, however minor, carries with it the anxiety of facing the unknown. Every transition stirs up memories or "memories in feeling" (Klein) about other losses and earlier fearful beginnings.

Many courses at the Tavistock Clinic begin with some time being set aside for students to reflect, as a group, on their feelings about starting a new course in a new institution. Isca Salzberger-Wittenberg (Salzberger-Wittenberg, Henry, & Osborne, 1983) wrote in detail about the responses she remembered from a group of teachers. Reflections from a group of social workers recently followed a very similar track. The first few contributors spoke expansively about their excitement, their positive expectations, their belief that the course would offer them something exceptional. They were a little anxious perhaps, but full of hope. Others spoke defensively from the outset. What was the fuss about? They were adults not children. This was not the first course they had attended, and there was no reason to be anxious. Slowly, people began to take the risk of talking about their more primitive fears and anxieties. One woman admitted that she had walked towards the building, struggling with a desire to turn and run. Another said that she had taken the day off work with a bad headache and felt relieved to have the perfect excuse to stay at home and miss the first evening of the course. She had only just managed to coax herself out of the house. Somebody else spoke about having had difficulty deciding what to wear; she was sure everybody would be very smart. This prompted another woman to say that she thought everybody would be thin. Yet another said she thought everybody would be cleverer than she! A male student said that he had been very worried that he might be the only man among a group of women, but then very honestly added that he was a bit disappointed to see that this was not the case—there were four other men! One woman felt sure that her acceptance letter had been sent in error and that she would find her name was not on the list. This led another to admit that she was even worried that she would not find her way around the building.

Where does all this begin? Psychoanalytic literature would suggest that the experience of birth is the first, hugely significant transition from one state of being to another. Infants arrive with more, or less, ease into a world that is entirely strange to them. They are bombarded by sounds and sensations and do not have the apparatus to make sense of them. At this point, they are completely dependent on the people who greet them and care for them. They begin a journey through infancy and childhood which is a complex interaction between their natural endowment (personality and genetic inheritance) and their environment. From the moment of birth (and, indeed, in utero), babies differ. Some are vigorous and protesting, others are passive and uncomplaining. It is not simply a matter of some parents being "better" at parenting than others. Some babies allow themselves to be parented, and some make it extremely difficult. The child who is fortunate enough to make a good "fit" with his mother or primary caregiver in the early months is likely to be better able to manage his first experiences of separation and, thereafter, to learn.

Weaning is often identified as the prototype for later experiences of separation. After weaning may come greater and more prolonged separations, with mothers going out, introducing alternative caregivers into the home, returning to work, leaving their child with a child-minder or in a nursery. If you watch a small toddler who has experienced a well-negotiated weaning and who has been introduced to the world in careful stages, you will see him making more and more adventurous forays away from his mother to explore his surroundings. At first he goes back often, for a cuddle or for verbal reassurance. As time goes on, he learns that she is still there on his return and he moves a little further away, perhaps looking back over his shoulder to check, but not needing to be in such close physical proximity. The child who has been led to believe that the world is a welcoming and fascinating place will be eager to explore it, so long as his secure base is there for him to return to.

This pattern does not really change as life and development move on. We all rely on a secure base to return to. Psychoanalytic thinking would suggest that the secure base, as one moves through childhood and towards adulthood, is increasingly an *internal* phenomenon. Experiences of containment and of well-managed separations are internalized, introjected, in a way that provides the individual with a good internal object, a secure and flexible inner world.

An autistic patient, an adolescent boy of 16, was able to say something about what it was like for him to live without this kind of inner resource to draw on. He sees his survival as entirely dependent on the continuity of his external supports. I quote: "When I was little and people went out, I thought they would never come back." And again I quote: "My Daddy went to America. He is back now and he is not dead." In cognitive terms, this boy knows that he and the people who are close to him continue to exist even when they are apart, but he does not feel it to be so. His experience in the face of sudden separation is that of a helpless infant. He once described it as "Nothing and nobody there". Of course, this is a very extreme example. There are enormous variations in degree of feeling in the face of a transition, and for most people, most of the time, the feelings are not overwhelming. Most of us, most of the time, have a sense of our own continuity, a belief that we will "go on being" through a period of change. However, primitive feelings can get stirred up by what appear, on the surface, to be very ordinary changes.

Beginnings

The first day at school is a very significant milestone in every child's life. Children are often enthusiastic about becoming "big" boys and girls, but their excitement will be tinged with feelings of uncertainty. Will they manage? Will they be clever enough? Will they like the food? Will the teacher get cross with them? And the biggest worry of all—what is Mummy doing without them? Will she remember to come and collect them at the end of the day, and will they hate her for having left them? The parents' fears are not so very different: Will he be safe? Is he ready for it? Will he ever forgive us for sending him out of the home?

There have been many policy changes over the past years. A great deal of thought and planning goes into preparing children for their first experience of school and for each of the major transitions. This shift in policy is perhaps most evident at secondary transfer when children are taken to visit their new schools before the summer break. It is recognized that they need to be shown around and that they need adults and older pupils to be available to introduce them to new routines and to support them over the first few weeks. This is obviously a good development, but there is a danger that with it goes an idea that this kind of preparation can spare children all pain and anxiety. I recently heard about a little boy whose parents and nursery teachers had talked to him very sensitively about what it would be like to go to "big school". He did not seem reassured and became increasingly anxious as the day drew near. He eventually confided in his teacher. How could he go to big school when his parents said that they were waiting for his passport to arrive? What would he do if it did not come in time? For him, big school was like another country, far away and very foreign.

Major transitions

Major points of transition in the education system are timed to coincide, for the majority, with major developmental changes: with the move from young childhood into latency, from latency into adolescence, and from adolescence into young adulthood. Children moving from one part of the education system to the next are seen as moving on to the next stage of life. For many, however, the timing of school transitions are out of kilter with their development, and they are faced with the challenge of how to fit into a social and educational world for which they are not ready. There are children in primary school classes who are patently not ready for formal classroom learning, but who need longer to consolidate their development in play-based activity. Some latency children are catapulted into adolescence at secondary transfer whether or not they have reached puberty and whether or not they might benefit from a longer period in the relatively calm seas of latency. Adolescents leaving school for the world of work and parenthood are often ill equipped in terms of their emotional development. Children and young people who are in this predicament may be able to adapt, but they will be much more likely to do so if their teachers are alert to their situation and can make some sort of allowance for individual differences of this kind.

Smaller transitions

I want to draw attention at this point to many of the much smaller beginnings, endings, and transitions that are a feature of school life. Every day is full of them. Children arrive from home. They meet one familiar teacher in their class group and then perhaps move off to an assembly with the whole school community. Back to the classroom, one lesson, and then a change of room, of topic, of teacher. Then a break and the noise and confusion of the playground. Back to the classroom again, then the library, the gymnasium, the dinner hall, and so on. Suddenly, the day ends and they are turned out of the building. Even the most well-endowed and well-adjusted children can feel buffeted about by this kind of programme. The less robust simply cannot manage it. They need lots of warning, even of the smallest changes. Again, a recent example I heard of was of a six-year-old child who was suddenly very unsettled in school. He had managed the previous year perfectly well and was lively and happy at home. After much thought and discussion, his parents and teachers realized what it was that had changed. His class was now being taught by a job-share pair; half the week with one teacher, half with the other. His parents wanted him to be moved to a different class but were persuaded that this was not the best solution. Far better was to explain it to him in detail and to give him, and the rest of the class too, a clear calendar and daily reminders of who would be with them the next morning.

Continuity

The most common visible example of the way in which children learn to manage early separations and to develop an inner sense of safety or comfort is the "security blanket", or what Winnicott (1951) calls the "transitional object". Most, though not all, children develop a reliance on one particular item of clothing, blanket, teddy bear, which they carry with them and depend on as a kind of concrete representation of the security of their early relationship with their mother. This object is taken to bed to keep the child "safe" at night and may be carried around the house by day, out into the street, around the supermarket, and so forth. In many families these items are invested with enormous significance by parents and by siblings too. I remember one family, described by a student doing an infant observation, who were distraught about the loss of toddler Ben's favourite teddy. His 5-year-old brother was the most upset of all, and he generously offered his own teddy as a substitute. The family moved around as if on eggshells, waiting for the moment when Ben would notice the loss and collapse in distress. They felt sure he would not sleep and would refuse to leave the house without his teddy. In fact, Ben managed the situation without any particular difficulty, and it seemed to the observer that he was able to rely on his internal objects in negotiating the ordinary transitions of the day. He was pleased to see the teddy again when it was found, but it was not a matter of life and death. In this example, the teddy was genuinely a "symbol". For some children, the loss (or removal at nursery or in infant school) of their "comforter" feels catastrophic, as if they are actually being ripped away from their primary carer and cast into a void. For others, the favoured toy is carried into nursery to provide a symbolic reminder of home and is very often not needed once the transition has been made.

The use of objects to assist individuals and groups in making transitions persists throughout school life and beyond. Children try all kinds of manoeuvres to take items home at the end of the day or to carry things with them from one classroom to another. The children who insist on bringing their favourite toy from home or who seem unable to resist wearing forbidden clothing or jewellery may not be simply "showing off" or "flouting the rules".

They may be demonstrating a need to surround themselves with concrete reminders of home and of other aspects of their life. It is always surprising to see much older children slipping a teddy or similar object into their luggage for a school trip, and one only has to look at the array of so-called mascots that adorn desks in an examination room to see that these "props" re-emerge at times of stress or anxiety.

The current preoccupation among children, adolescents, and adults with the mobile phone is an interesting phenomenon in relation to the management of separation and transition. Certainly, it has replaced the "trainer" as the badge of designer "cred" among adolescents, but I want to suggest that it also fulfils a much more significant function. The idea that you can be in touch with your loved ones, your "secure base", or your reliable "external objects" almost at any time is a revolutionary one. On trains and in the street, one can see how it is used to erase the experience of being separate, of being "out of touch", while in transition from one situation to another. People can now talk to their partners, families, or friends as they walk through airports or as their trains leave the station. The mobile phone plays into our desire to deny or to eradicate the anxiety of these separations, to postpone the moment of saying goodbye, and to anticipate the moment of reunion. I recently witnessed a man on a train talking throughout the journey to his wife or partner. In the last few minutes of the journey it became clear that she was driving the car to meet him at the station, and he talked her into the car park, rather as air-traffic control might talk a plane in to land! He was still talking to her as he rushed along the station platform towards the ticket barrier.

The growth of email and texts as means of communication perhaps carries with it some of the same supposed benefits. Instead of having to wait for a letter to reach its destination and then to spend some days anticipating a response, we can now fire out an email or text and get an almost simultaneous response. The speed is convenient certainly, but the immediacy perhaps also serves to create an illusion of no waiting, no separation, no distance, and no frustration.

Endings

Leaving a school is a major event for teachers and students alike. There may be enthusiasm for whatever is to come next, but there will also be sadness and a sense of loss. The loss of a school community, and particularly of more intimate relationships within the school, is a very significant loss. It stirs up conscious and unconscious memories of earlier losses—weaning, starting school, bereavements, and so on. Children (and adults) develop very different styles of managing an ending. It is perhaps less common than it used to be, but some teachers are still guilty of leaving their posts without telling the children they are going. Not so long ago I heard about a head teacher who insisted that none of the staff who were leaving mention anything to their classes. She justified this by saying that she did not want to worry the parents about a high staff turnover, but it became clear that she did not want to have to cope with the anticipated outpouring of feeling from the children, nor perhaps to face her own feelings of anger, disappointment, and rejection.

The end-of-year party or the leaver's concert may be an important ritual, marking a rite of passage that has been thought about and prepared for. It may, on the other hand, be a defensive manoeuvre to make sure that nobody dwells on sad feelings. We all have ways of trying not to notice an ending, or at least to deny the element of loss. The same can happen in schools on Friday afternoons. Children's deteriorating behaviour is not just tiredness and excitement about the weekend; many of them want to avoid painful feelings of loss: of the structure of the school day, of relationships with peers and teachers, and so forth. Teachers and pupils often collude by dismantling the structure early, with Friday afternoons being given over to "choices", "golden time", "games", and so on. The adult version of this for some groups of teachers is to adjourn to the pub on Friday nights. They have been longing for Friday but somehow cannot go their separate ways. Leaving at the end of term can be even more difficult, however much they are looking forward to going away on holiday. I do not think that teachers suffer from illness in the holidays *only* because they are exhausted after a term's work. Holidays, however welcome, are a disruption to routine and a separation from many familiar supports.

In a truancy scheme in London in the 1980s, the adolescents introduced me to the full range of possibilities when it came to the ways in which they left the unit. Many left early, weeks before their legal school-leaving date. Some simply slipped away without a word, while others provoked a confrontation and stormed out. Some managed to manoeuvre us into excluding them and left triumphant that they had proved we were rubbish, just like school. A few found jobs to go to, but sadly many of the boys were arrested for acts of delinquency and went into youth custody. Sadly also, many of the girls became pregnant just before the end of term and left believing their future to be mapped out for them.

The few who did stay till the end did not make it easy for themselves or for the staff. They would beg for treats and outings and then stay at home in bed. They would accuse the staff of neglect. They would call the staff "failed" teachers because they were not in proper schools. They would deny the ending altogether, planning elaborate reunions which would never take place. Many could not leave on the appointed date. Visits would start the following day. Some would visit occasionally, some weekly, some daily. One girl visited every day, forcing the teachers, eventually, to tell her that she had to reduce the frequency of her visits. She then never came back.

What is the unconscious agenda here? What was the meaning of these behaviours? These were children who did not attend school. Many had been rejected by school, or at least they believed themselves to have been rejected. Most came from homes where the parents were actively neglectful, abusive, or simply so depressed and despairing that they were ineffective as parents. These young people had no experience of an adult helping them through a transition, helping them to manage a loss, or really to look forward to a new opportunity. However much work went into trying to steer them towards a better kind of ending, the unconscious sabotage almost always took over.

The same kind of thing would happen when they faced the loss of a good experience such as an outing. Things would often go wrong on the journey home, with the group suddenly falling out with each other or with us, enabling them to storm off home without a backward glance. I remember one very distressing experience with a group who had enjoyed a thoroughly good day out in Margate. They had been cheerful and appreciative until it was time to go home. They deliberately missed the booked train, and we, the staff group, were angry and accused them of being selfish and thoughtless. They had all run out of spending money, and we refused to buy drinks or food. We had all travelled out together, but we now put ourselves in a separate carriage, like parents who wanted privacy after a difficult day with the children. They reacted to our giving up on them by vandalizing their carriage, smashing lights, and ripping up seats. The result was that we were all delayed for many hours by the ensuing investigation, and everyone went home feeling shocked and miserable.

These are extreme examples. What about the more ordinary school population? What is the unconscious agenda on leaving a school or, indeed, on leaving one class to go on to another? The following list of possibilities is not exhaustive, but I hope it is clear how these ideas relate to early experience and to aspects of the relationship between infant and caregiver.

- Is the teacher relieved that I am going? Did she hate me?
- Will she remember me? Will she miss me?
- Did she like our class best? Did she like me best?
- Will her next class be cleverer?
- Will I like my next teacher? Will she like me?
- Will I cope?
- Will my old teacher be alright after I have gone?
- Did we damage her? Were we too badly behaved?

And for the teacher:

- Are they glad to be going?
- Will they like the next teacher better?
- Will they remember me?
- Did I teach them properly?

- Will they pass or fail?
- What will the next lot be like? Will I cope? etc.

The similarity between these two sets of anxieties is striking, as is the resonance with the thoughts verbalized by the group of social workers quoted at the beginning of the chapter. These kinds of preoccupations are exceedingly common and can be managed by most children, teachers, and schools most of the time. However, an understanding of the significance of change and transition for all of us in ordinary circumstances can help teachers to notice and support those children for whom it is a major area of difficulty. Some very young children really do need help to make the most routine transitions. They need time to prepare for a change of activity, they need reassurance that the room and the teacher will be there when they return from the playground. They need to be able to sit on the same spot on the carpet until they feel brave enough to move. Later on, they need a great deal of preparation for holiday breaks, for moving up into a new class, for transferring to secondary school. It is sometimes assumed that these are children whose parents have not been able to allow them to grow up and separate, and teachers very readily speak of overdependency, of enmeshed relationships, of clingy children or clingy parents. It may be that there is a shared reluctance to give up the closeness of early experience. However, it may also be that there have been events in the family which have left parents and children susceptible to extreme anxiety at times of change. Illness, death, divorce, redundancy, dislocation, and homelessness all challenge the individual's capacity to hold on to a sense of continuity and challenge the school's capacity to contain anxiety.

CHAPTER SEVEN

Understanding behaviour: insight in the classroom and the value of observation

Teachers who face classes of twenty to thirty-five children, hour after hour and day after day, often protest that the kind of understanding offered in this volume is all very interesting, but of limited use to them. Their working lives, they say, are such that there is absolutely no room for anything extra. How can they possibly attend to the needs of every single child? How can they be expected to attend to the children's emotional development as well as to delivering the National Curriculum, completing all the paperwork, and reaching their targets? Classroom teachers sometimes join together, taking up a besieged and beleaguered position, envying those who have time for reflection, and projecting all the insight into the so-called experts. A split opens up between those who are preoccupied with having to "manage" behaviour and those who seek to "understand" the child.

Observation

Many teachers acknowledge that they feel they cannot afford to open themselves up to the emotional experience of children or the reality of their home lives for fear of being overwhelmed. Perhaps this is one of the reasons why so many interventions in schools follow a strictly behavioural line, setting targets and relying on systems of reward and punishment. Much of what goes on in classrooms under the heading of "observation" is geared towards achieving objectivity in making assessments of children's behaviour. When somebody sets about observing a child or group of children, the aim is usually to isolate particular behaviours, quantify them, and identify triggers. The observer's purpose is to try to understand something about cause and effect in order to make an appropriate intervention. Observation of teachers is conducted in much the same way, with carefully constructed checklists designed to measure the success of the lesson and identify areas for improvement.

The belief is that an observer needs to be at a distance from the action, insulated against the emotional temperature and able to focus and record the data accurately. The method I am describing here is rather different. It is not done from a distance, nor with the aid of formalized tick-sheets. It depends on the observer being involved in the unfolding scene and being able to engage with the experience in an attentive, open, and thoughtful way. It invites the observer to reflect on his or her own emotional responses as well as the evidence of his or her eyes and ears. It introduces the possibility that the observer continue to observe in detail, even when engaged in ordinary work tasks.

Work discussion

Work discussion is a central part of the Emotional Factors in Learning and Teaching course as well as of many other professional development and pre-clinical courses at the Tavistock Clinic. The task is as follows. Students are expected to write a detailed description of a period of about an hour in their place of work and to bring that account to the seminar for discussion. The write-up has to be done after the event, without recourse to notes made at the time, or to aids such as audio recordings. The students are encouraged to remember and write down as much detail as possible and to include descriptions of their own thoughts and emotional responses. In fact, they are usually surprised by how much detail they can remember. They can choose to write about a sequence of events in the classroom, a lunch break, an outing, a meeting with a parent—in short, any aspect of the working day that raises questions in their minds and which they would like to think about further.

I have written elsewhere (Youell, 1999a, 2005) about the psycho-analytic observational stance and the way in which it challenges professional's familiar "objective" ways of observing. On courses at the Tavistock Clinic, teachers and others are asked to observe in an open and profoundly "subjective" way. They are asked to become emotionally as well as intellectually engaged, to be open to the feeling states of others as well as to reflect on their own. A good memory helps but is not enough. An accurate narrative does not of itself bring a situation to life, and students are encouraged to use vivid, descriptive language.

The seminar leader is a child psychotherapist, and it is here that the expertise of the teachers in their field comes together with the knowledge and experience of the clinician. The group work together to reach some understanding of aspects of the interactions, focusing on the emotional experience and the un-conscious communication between teacher and pupil. It is the attention to the impact on the observer—the countertransfer-ence—that distinguishes this kind of activity from other meth-ods of observation. The purpose of the seminar discussion is to enhance the teachers' understanding of their pupil or pupils but also to support them in thinking about aspects of their own emo-tional experience as well as of their professional practice within their particular role.

Observation and insight

Teachers embarking on the course usually say that their motiva-tion for doing so is a desire to understand more about pupils who challenge them in some way. They want to know why children behave the way they do and why they, as teachers, feel so puzzled or troubled by what they do not understand or cannot manage in the classroom. They are preoccupied with the children and young people who do not learn and who cannot seem to make use of the help that is on offer. They enrol on the course because they are interested in "emotional factors" but are often still surprised by the absence of an emphasis on strategies and solutions. Some are frustrated by the fact that they sometimes go away from a seminar with more questions than answers. There is often a fantasy that a detailed history of the pupil's home life and school career (which is not required) would provide the missing pieces of the puzzle. There may also be a fantasy that the seminar leader is deliberately withholding insight.

Engaging fully with the task of work discussion requires that participants be willing to try to reflect on their own emotional responses and share their thoughts with their fellow students. This can be very difficult at first, particularly when they fear that their reactions to some children are not worthy of a committed, professional teacher. They find it hard to admit to feelings of dislike or intolerance and are understandably reluctant to describe disorganized lessons or to write about their own fears of losing control. Some course members bring descriptions of their very "best" lessons, others write about a pupil, a class, or the school institution in a way that invites the group to agree that they cannot be expected to teach in such circumstances. Alternatively, the seminar can become a kind of confessional, with all assumed failings set out for all to see, as if the presenter is seeking confirmation that she is a "bad" teacher. It takes time to establish a setting in which there can be a genuine space for reflection and exchange of ideas. When this is achieved, fear of unwelcome exposure or judgement is replaced by an expectation that projected states of mind can be made conscious in the process of gathering "evidence" about what is really going on in a teacher–pupil interaction.

The work-discussion seminar is the quintessence of the notion of "learning from experience", with didactic input offered only in making links between observational material and psychoanalytic theory. The crucial element of learning is the way in which reflection on the detail of the observation, with due attention being paid to the teacher's emotional responses, can illuminate aspects of the conscious and unconscious experience. This, in turn, can lead the teacher to a better understanding of how best to help the child within the parameters of the teacher's role.

A brief example from the first seminar of one academic year: In the absence of a written observation, I asked if anybody would be able to talk extemporaneously about a situation that troubled them. A male teacher stepped in and rather apologetically presented a problem he had with two of his class. These two children, both aged 10, had taken to coming into school early to help him prepare the classroom (clean the whiteboard, sharpen pencils, set out equipment, and so on). Both were very reliable, and he was reluctant to give up the help. However, the truth was that he found Johnny's presence unobtrusive but Kerry's deeply irritating. He was puzzled by this, as the two children were providing exactly the same service. In the seminar, he was encouraged to say more about both children and to explore the nature of his irritation. The group heard that Johnny was a small, quiet boy who got on with whatever task was assigned to him. Kerry, by contrast, was talkative and full of ideas as to how things could be organized. Members of the seminar group asked about how these two children behaved at other times, and the presenter said that Johnny found the playground noisy and threatening, although he was not unpopular in his own class. He made no particular demands on his teacher, but the teacher had noticed that Johnny became anxious at points in the day when they moved to other parts of the school and would stay close to his side in the assembly hall. Kerry was always nearby. She sat close to her teacher's feet on the carpet at story time and was always at the front of the line. Her hand shot up in response to questions, and she was the first to volunteer to do errands, such as taking the register to the office. The presenter described an interaction that had taken place in the car park at eight o'clock that morning. He had been climbing out of his car, bleary-eyed and preoccupied, when Kerry had popped up as if from nowhere, offering to carry his bags. He was deeply ashamed of his response, which had been to snap at the child—"No thanks! For goodness sake, go to the playground." He admitted that he had actually felt like sweeping Kerry aside.

Talking about it in the seminar, it became clear that Kerry's way of helping was somehow intrusive and controlling. It emerged that her mother was a school secretary, and the group speculated that she was in identification with a kind of indispensable PA (or wife?). The identification was "adhesive" in character (see chapter 2). Her teacher felt she somehow wanted to stick herself to him in a way that felt quite different from Johnny's need to be close. In other words, Kerry was protecting herself from feeling some of the anxiety of being a child who is faced with learning from a more experienced and mature adult.

Of course, the insight afforded by this discussion does not of itself solve the problem. The teacher was genuinely shaken by the strength of his hostile response to Kerry and wondered what he had brought to the situation from his own internal world. The group felt there was something about gender differences which would be worthy of further exploration, and there was disagreement as to how the two children might best be helped to break the early morning habit and move out into the playground. There was much further work to be done. However, the point here is simply that bringing the issue to the seminar enabled the teacher to identify significant differences between the two children. At first glance, their behaviour was the same, but the internal drivers were revealed to be very different.

This impromptu presentation proved to be a valuable introduction to the benefits of attending to the feelings evoked in the teacher as well as to the behaviour of the pupil. Students very often express surprise that the seminar discussion helps as much as it does, given that the aim is not to identify strategies as such. They often come back a week after a presentation, saying that they have made significant progress with a child—in fact, they are convinced the child must have known they were being discussed! There is nothing magical about this. Given the nature of containment (chapters 1 and 2), it seems entirely logical that if the teacher's anxiety has been contained by the seminar group, she will be better able to contain the anxiety of her pupil. Pupils know when their teachers are receptive and thoughtful. It should also be made clear that if this way of observing makes sense to teachers, it becomes part of their ordinary working life. If there is no seminar group, teachers will check their ideas about what they observe against the experience of colleagues or will carry on a dialogue within themselves.

I conclude this chapter with a fuller example from a work-discussion seminar. The presenter is working in a Pupil Referral Unit (PRU) for adolescents.

I am "key teacher" for Ryan and have the job of trying to get him back into his mainstream school. He is fifteen years old. He is tall, thin, and blonde . . . with very lively eyes and a charming smile which he uses to disarm people when they try to tell him off. He can be horribly rude and enjoys winding the other kids up by "cussing" their mothers.

This observation took place immediately after the lunch break. My colleague told me that there had been an incident at lunchtime. Tracey had been talking about how Ryan always took huge portions of pudding only to throw it away. Today, the pudding happened to be everybody's favourite, Arctic Roll. My colleague asked them not to be greedy as there were a lot of children in the PRU that day. As the plates were passed round, Ryan realized he had got a very small slice. The other kids were laughing and Tracey muttered "Shame." Ryan pushed the plate back across the table, turning very red in the face. He threw his spoon at Tracey and walked out, saying he was not going to eat with a "load of morons". To everyone's surprise, he returned for afternoon lessons, having made peace with Tracey in the break.

When I walked into the classroom to teach the lesson, I told the group to turn off the music and asked Ryan to take the cassette recorder back to the office (which is next to this room). He was sitting, looking glum, muttering under his breath. I repeated my request, wondering to myself why I had chosen to ask him. He refused and went through the full range of usual responses, "I didn't get it out", "I didn't listen to it", "Why me?", and finally, "I'm no Joey." I asked him why he was making such a scene and reminded him that he had made a show of himself at lunchtime over something just as silly. I immediately heard my words as provocative and regretted having made such a public reference to an earlier incident. As a rule, I try not to refer back to incidents once they have been resolved, especially when I wasn't even there myself! My words hung in the air as Ryan stiffened, and I glanced anxiously around the table at the other kids. They were sitting very still but beginning to giggle. Ryan repeated that he was not here to fetch and carry. We were supposed to be teachers, and he did not need to be taught to carry things and we could all just "fuck off".

I reminded him that swearing was not allowed in the PRU and said that my request was no big deal and I could just as well have asked somebody else. "Why don't you, then?" I answered that he had now made an issue of it and that I had to insist because otherwise he was saying that he could just please himself about everything. I said that he knew the rule was that they did what we asked, so long as it was a reasonable request. He looked at me challengingly and said "Would you go to the shop for me if I asked? No. So why should I carry things around for you?" I felt my face redden and my heart began to beat faster as I wondered how I could get out of this mess.

The other kids were beginning to join in, encouraged by his bravado and maybe sensing that I was losing control. "Go for it, Ryan", "You tell her, mate", "They think they're something don't they?" and so on. One of the girls tried, "Ryan, just take the fucking thing. What's your problem?" Another said mockingly, "Are you going to let her win? Oh, I'm sorry, I forgot, she's the boss round here." David said he wanted to get on with the lesson, and everyone rounded on him and called him a "creep" and a "teacher's pet". Somebody suggested he fancied me, and then they all got the giggles, David included.

I felt rising panic as I floundered around for the right tactic. Trying to sound calm, I said that Ryan either took the radio as asked or he would have to leave. He beamed at this and asked where he had to go. Home? The pub? He was now standing, staring at me with a look of utter determination. His eyes were shining. The others began a slow handclap. I felt very stupid and wished that I had found a way to get out of the room with him before having this confrontation. As I opened my mouth to tell him to go, he got up, pushed his chair back noisily, and went over to the cassette player. I thought he might throw it at me or smash it on the floor. I stood very still and repeated that he needed to decide and that I hoped he would find a way to stay. I felt as if my voice was shaking. He lifted the radio above his head but then said, "Only joking", tucked it under his arm, and set off jauntily for the office, throwing me a glance and then a beaming smile.

I suggested the rest of the group settle down and get out their work. Ryan was gone for about ten minutes, but I decided not to make an issue of it. When he came back, he ignored renewed jibes from the group and settled very quickly, working much harder than usual, asking for help and insisting that I mark his book at the end of the lesson. He went out at break with a cheery, "Bye, miss." I was baffled by this turnaround but was glad I hadn't thrown him out.

Discussion

The seminar group was also baffled by Ryan's climbdown and had to work hard to make sense of the sequence of events and see-saw of emotions. The presenter said that she could understand something of Ryan's experience over the pudding. The most emotionally deprived children were often the ones to take the biggest helpings of food. They were often also the ones to leave a little on their plates, as if to reassure themselves that they had plenty of everything and need never feel hungry or depleted. By bringing up the issue of greed and waste, her colleague unwittingly created a situation in which somebody would be bound to feel humiliated. The presenter laughed at the way she had been able to see the mistake her colleague had made but then jumped in and made a very similar one just a few minutes later, putting Ryan straight back under the spotlight.

Still sensitive following the lunchtime humiliation, Ryan experienced what was an ordinary request as an intolerable insult and desperately tried to find a way to prove he was "no Joey". The rest of the group could again project into him, egging him on against the teacher who for most of them, in the transference, seemed to have become either a depriving maternal figure or a completely ineffectual one. Emboldened by their support, Ryan was able to project his feelings of stupidity into the teacher, who was, by this time, feeling very stupid and very stuck herself. Once the feeling of being stuck was firmly lodged in her, he really did seem to find room for manoeuvre and things shifted.

The seminar group wondered if this situation had resolved itself in a helpful way or if it had depended on the teacher being humiliated. Surely it was not good for Ryan to feel better at the teacher's expense? He had won. The group got very caught up in the account as being a story of a confrontation, a battle of wills, that must have a winner and a loser. Ryan had been allowed to get away with swearing—so the teacher had lost. However, he had eventually taken the tape recorder, so maybe she had won? She confirmed that she felt relieved but not humiliated. Some of the group felt that the presenter should have dealt with the behaviour of the rest of the group and, in particular, should have supported David in getting on with the lesson.

What actually seems to have facilitated a peaceful outcome was the observer's capacity to go on thinking in the heat of the moment. She was not simply reacting to his provocation, but was reflecting on her feelings and trying to think of a way to help Ryan and herself out of the impasse. Her struggle to think creatively un-doubtedly conveyed itself to Ryan, who was then able to take steps to extricate himself and to reward her for her efforts by returning to her lesson and working hard. His ten-minute absence was pos-sibly a statement of defiance in case his peers thought him weak, or maybe he needed time to calm down fully before returning to the classroom. His behaviour in the rest of the lesson was not that of an arrogant, triumphant bully but was that of an appreciative pupil.

Summary

An accusation often levelled against psychoanalytic thinking is that it absolves individuals of responsibility for their actions, that it explains away bad behaviour in terms of a child's history, or worse, by blaming parents. The aim of this chapter has been to demonstrate just how inaccurate this is, by mapping out the ways in which rigorous psychoanalytically informed observation can be utilized by classroom teachers. The usefulness falls into two overlapping categories. First, there is the matter of what can be achieved minute by minute in the classroom if teachers and others working in the setting are open to unconscious communication and are able to think about it with reference to theoretical ideas of personality development and group dynamics. Second, there is the relief to be gained in being able to reflect on one's own experience as a teacher and to understand something about it—that is, to be able to separate out what belongs to whom and what one can and cannot change.

CHAPTER EIGHT

Special educational needs

This chapter focuses on some of the issues involved in working with children with special educational needs, particularly within the context of mainstream schools. Policies of inclusion over the past ten to twenty years have resulted in a proliferation in the number of professionals working in schools. Special Educational Needs Coordinators (SENCO) now manage large teams of workers: classroom assistants, individual support teachers, learning mentors, home–school liaison workers, behaviour support teams (BEST), parent volunteers, and others. Teachers have to become accustomed to working alongside these additional members of staff, each of whom has a very specific job description. The system often works extremely well, but it creates its own demands, and one of these is a very high level of cooperation and understanding among the adults.

The term "special educational needs" covers a huge range of difficulties. I am aware that as soon as I use the word "difficulty", I open myself up to the accusation that I have misunderstood the spirit of the inclusion policy, which is based on a wish that children with special needs should not be viewed as difficult or problematic. They should be seen as having something particular to offer the school community. Very few people would argue with the notion that all children have a right to appropriate educational opportunity, nor with the idea that being part of a genuinely mixed-ability school population is the best social education for children. However, the fact is that children with identified special needs are children who require something different and extra and, as such, present schools with a challenge. It is also a fact that Special Education legislation covers widely different and unrelated areas of special need. Some "special needs" are organic, some entirely physical, some psychological or emotional, some environmental, some temporary, some chronic.

I will begin with an exploration of some of the issues that arise when there is a clearly identified and highly visible disability. I hope that the relevance of these ideas to thinking about other forms of "special need" will become apparent.

Children with mental and physical disabilities

Special schools do still exist. A few conditions are recognized as demanding such specialist care that they cannot be managed in mainstream settings. This is not the case in some European countries, notably Italy, where all children have to be catered for within community schools. My purpose here is not to write about special schools but to look in detail at some of the dynamics that are present in mainstream schools when staff are seeking to work together in support of children who need particular kinds of attention. I shall draw some examples from a short course offered in Italy to "*sostegni*"—experienced support teachers working with children with disabilities in mainstream schools. The degrees of disability were sometimes extreme, but many of the issues confronting the Italian teachers are exactly those that beset support teachers and classroom assistants in this country.

Cooperative working

It is probably impossible for two or more adults to work together in a classroom without issues of rivalry emerging. Who is in charge?

Who is the better teacher? Whom do the children prefer? Even where the adults have been aware of these tensions and have come to some understanding, a child with special educational needs is likely to get under their defences and expose splits between them. Children receiving extra support are likely, in the transference, to endow one teacher with positive qualities and the other with negative. They often either reject the attention of the support teacher, remaining "loyal" to their class teacher, or they idealize the "special" teacher in ways that can undermine the confidence and the authority of the class teacher. The class teacher can feel that the visiting teacher has the easy job, gets all the rewards, and then leaves her to pick up the pieces (very like the mother who is left to deal with the aftermath of father's contact visit). This kind of rivalry can lead class teachers, in turn, to treat visiting teachers very badly, ignoring them or expecting them to take on all kinds of menial tasks. Some of these difficulties, though not all, arise as a result of undigested or indigestible feelings about the child with a special need or about the special need itself.

Ambivalence

I shall illustrate some points about the teacher's experience with an extreme example that comes from a work-discussion seminar where a support teacher in Italy was describing her work in a mainstream school, supporting a boy with multiple disabilities. This 13-year-old boy, Roberto, was deaf and blind and had a physical condition that meant that he could not control his bladder or bowel and could only walk with assistance. He made strange noises and hit out at anybody who came within range. His support teacher had been with him for several years, and she was one of the few people he would allow to come close. Indeed, with puberty he had become increasingly keen to hold her very close and tried to get her to lie down with him on the mattress where he spent some hours of each school day. In the seminar, the support teacher put an enormous amount of energy into insisting that her pupil was "happy" and was enjoying school. She claimed that she loved the boy and thought his mother neglectful. She also said that the negative responses of the class teachers and able-bodied children in the school enraged her. She insisted that her work was rewarding, in spite of the fact that the boy's disability was such that he could offer her very little in the way of feedback or appreciation.

When I suggested that being with this child day after day might not be entirely rewarding, there was an outcry from the whole group. Did I not understand how committed they all were to the children they worked with? I persisted in questioning what seemed to be an over-idealized picture and wondered why it was so difficult to express any ambivalence about their students. The presenter eventually admitted that, recently, she had been waking with a heavy heart and had to force herself to go to work. She had felt very guilty about it and so had told no one. Given this lead, the group felt able to voice some of their own negative feelings and to see that the reluctance to acknowledge them might arise from a fear of being overwhelmed by feelings of distaste or hatred for the children, or a fear of losing all sense of hope and self-worth. It then became possible to think about how this might mirror the experience of the children themselves and their parents, who similarly feel compelled to deny negative feelings. If Roberto could not reward his teacher for her devoted care, what must have been the experience for his mother?

For the Italian teachers attending this course, the seminar became a safe space in which they could express the full range of feelings without fear of lasting censure. This was partly a result of getting to know and trust the other group members and finding a lot of common ground. However, more importantly, with increasing confidence in the reflective space of the seminar came a growing understanding of psychoanalytic theory. The concepts of projection, transference, and countertransference release one from feeling that one is solely responsible for all negativity and failure in a therapeutic or a teaching relationship. Being able to think about what might be being projected into the support teacher, or into the student, enabled the group to move away from a simple culture of success, on the one hand, and failure or blame, on the other. Understanding the countertransference and becoming able to think about what belongs to oneself (in terms of emotional preoccupation and fixed behavioural patterns) and what is a communication from the pupil helps the support teacher to begin to make sense of what can be very powerful emotional experiences.

The meaning of disability

What does it mean for a child to have a disability, and what does it mean for a teacher or support worker to have chosen to work with children with disabilities? The response of special-needs teachers is often defensive. They are justifiably proud of the work they do, but, as illustrated in the example above, there is a tendency to idealize the *special* child as if he is immune from many of the emotions that beset the rest of us or as if he must be protected from all criticism. Support teachers can all too readily get into a position in which they and their student are in a kind of mutually idealizing twosome, projecting all the dissatisfaction and frustration into those around them. In this position, the support teacher can see herself as the child's only ally, becoming critical of the parents and the mainstream teachers.

Another tendency in those who work with special-needs children is to become identified with the special need themselves. The support teacher becomes the adult who is on the edge of the institution, isolated from colleagues in the same way as her pupil is isolated from peers. She can become weighed down with the disappointment and despair projected into her from the pupil himself or from the pupil's family and can become hopeless about the future. I remember teaching in an off-site unit for school-refusers and very quickly becoming identified with the client group, almost phobic about going into the huge, noisy schools and feeling that I had effectively excluded myself from a mainstream career. The pupils used to ask us periodically what we had done wrong to end up in the unit—why weren't we able to be "proper teachers"?

Secondary handicap

"Secondary handicap" is a phrase that was coined by Valerie Sinason (1986) to describe the way in which the child with a physical or learning disability further handicaps himself by conforming to the low expectations that others have of him. She highlights the way in which, in extreme cases, the child with a disability "goes stupid" rather than struggles with the reality of what he can and cannot manage. She writes about the way in which children with special needs are acutely tuned in to any disappointment or despair in their carers and teachers. A cycle can get set up between teacher and pupil in which the child underperforms, the teacher lowers her expectations, and the child responds accordingly.

This unconscious collusion between teacher and pupil was a theme that emerged very clearly during the course in Italy. Over time, it became possible to support the demoralized workers in setting manageable targets that would challenge the child and provide a sense of achievement. Many presentations showed the way in which some of the children with special needs had managed to convince everyone around them that they could do very little for themselves and that to expect them to struggle with some ordinary tasks would be an act of cruelty. In some cases, it was simply a matter of setting some ordinary limits on behaviour. When a child is suffering real physical and mental pain—as many of the pupils described in the seminars were—it is very easy to fall into the trap of believing that the child must be indulged and never frustrated. Again, the teachers found it hard to accept that they were not being cruel if they expected ordinary politeness from their pupils or if they demanded that if the child could manage ordinary tasks, such as dressing or cutting up his own food, he should do so.

Coming to terms with disability

One of the most painful aspects of life for children with a disability is coming to terms with their own situation and managing feelings of envy and resentment about the capacities of their peers. Lynda Miller (2004) writes about the way in which awareness of their own difficulties begins, for many, with awareness of the disappointment in their parents' eyes. She states that if the family and others caring for the child do not manage to contain the child's anxiety, a harshly critical system can be put in place that is very resistant to change by the time the child is in formal education. She writes:

> The formation of a harsh and judgemental superego will generate the very low self-esteem that one often finds when working therapeutically with learning-disabled adolescents. It is this powerfully negative view of themselves that leads learning-disabled adolescents to readily take on their societal role as

excluded, unwanted outsiders, preferably remaining unseen by others. It may also impede their capacities to develop and to learn because the fundamental sense of self is damaged and is felt to be incapable of healthy cognitive growth. [pp. 84–85]

The inclusion policy in Britain's schools is clearly designed to minimize the isolation of the disabled child. In many ways it achieves this end, fostering awareness and tolerance in the school population as a whole. (For a fuller discussion of group dynamics, see chapters 9 and 10.) However, it also means that the child with the disability is constantly reminded of the difference between himself and his more able peers. This can lead special-needs children into taking up defensively omnipotent positions in which they deny their difficulties, but more often it results in a distressing level of self-criticism bordering on despair. The support worker is usually the one who has to hold on to the hope for the child and who has the responsibility of structuring work tasks in ways that will maximize progress and enhance self-esteem.

Very often it is the support teachers who fulfil a vital function for their pupils by being the one who observes them in detail and who seeks to understand the unconscious communications in relation to issues of coming to terms with disability. If the worker can contain anxiety and can tolerate the sometimes powerful communications of envy, anger, and resentment, she can begin to help the child to work through some of these emotions and develop a more realistic sense of his own self-worth.

Developmental stages

One of the benefits of inclusion for support teachers is the fact that in a mainstream classroom they stay in touch with ordinary expectations and are reminded that many of the tasks involved in the stages of development apply just as much to their pupils as to the rest of the population. The Italian teachers talked about the tendency in those who do not work closely with special-needs children to see disability as halting development and to fail to notice changes, whether physical or emotional. Teachers gave examples of how they felt that they did notice and celebrate developmental achievements and how aware they were that there has to be a flexible model that allows for developmental milestones coming late or in an idiosyncratic order.

There was a great deal of discussion, however, about the anxiety that accompanies the early signs of puberty in children with severe disabilities. Parents rarely prepare themselves or their children for this major change, because they fear the impact of burgeoning sexuality and the accompanying increase in emotionality and physical strength. It also, perhaps, heralds the beginning of a period in which parents have to make painful decisions about the future care of their grown children. Some teachers acknowledged that they tried to ignore their pupils' masturbatory behaviour or preferred to think of expressions of physical affection as entirely devoid of sexual intent. Adolescents with disabilities, like all others, need to be helped to manage their sexuality and to conduct themselves within socially acceptable limits. At the same time, some of the elements of adolescence can be welcomed and fostered, with young people being encouraged to express their opinions and to make choices for themselves where possible.

Young people with less severe disabilities often report that they were comfortable in their primary schools, where they felt themselves to be genuinely part of the community, only to have their worlds turned upside down by the transfer to secondary school. Secondary schools are bigger and noisier, and there is a requirement that pupils move around the building at speed, carrying quantities of books and equipment. There is also a very different atmosphere, the adolescents becoming preoccupied with their appearance, with fashion, with arrangements for their social lives, and so on. This can be a very painful experience for the individual who finds himself excluded from some or all of this experience. School placements often break down at this point, and the student is again faced with coming to terms with the restrictions imposed by his disability.

Relationships with parents

As indicated earlier in this chapter, the relationship that a school has with the parents of a disabled child can be complex. It is very common for rivalry to develop, with the school believing that it knows what is best for the child and becoming unduly critical of the mother, who is variously seen as neglectful or overindulgent. The mother, in turn, may see the school as failing in its task or as over-involved and interfering. Parents sometimes manage their own anger and disappointment by launching a campaign on behalf of their child, determined that they should not be deprived of any possible treatment or support. The Italian teachers admitted that they had not really thought about the experience of parents who give birth to a child with a physical handicap or whose child develops a learning disability later in childhood. It was helpful to think together about how the parents have to mourn the loss of the baby they had been expecting and to come to terms with the child they have instead. It was painful, but vitally important, to recognize that the parents have to manage feelings of hatred for their child as well as feelings of love and commitment. A simple reminder that teachers spend a few hours per day with the child whereas the family live with the difficulties day after day, year after year, can be salutary for teachers who are feeling critical of traumatized, exhausted, and demoralized parents.

On this theme, Trudy Klauber (1998), writing on working with parents of children with autistic spectrum disorder, draws attention to the fact that the parents are often suffering from a kind of post-traumatic stress disorder, reliving the trauma of the pre-diagnosis investigations and of the diagnosis itself. She writes about the way in which the child acts as a living reminder of this traumatic experience and that the subsequent guilt about their hatred for the child leads parents to overcompensate by devoting themselves unquestioningly to the child's demands. She underlines what was mentioned above in terms of the way in which a child with a disability can become a tyrant at home and/or at school, as those around him feel unable to challenge the assumption that he is too fragile or too vulnerable to accept normal limits.

Applications to work with other "special needs"

How useful is the foregoing discussion in thinking about the needs of children who do not have a visible disability but who need and receive additional support in mainstream schools? I shall finish by making a few further comments. Many of the dynamics described above occur between class teachers and support teachers, classroom assistants, parent volunteers, and other "visitors" to the mainstream school. The child who is identified as having "special needs" becomes a magnet for projections from teachers, support workers, and peers. Splits can open up between those who seek to foster the individual child's development and those who are charged with responsibility for the progress of the majority. The special need is all too easily seen as a nuisance, as a hindrance to the progress of the class as a whole, or, worse, as a drain on resources. This is particularly so, perhaps, when there is no diagnosed or diagnosable condition. It is therefore not surprising that many parents actively seek a label for their troubled or troublesome child.

The proliferation of diagnoses of dyslexia, dyspraxia, ADHD (Attention Deficit Hyperactivity Disorder), Semantic Pragmatic Disorder, Asperger's Syndrome, and so forth is not necessarily indicative of an increased incidence of these conditions. Seeking a label is sometimes a necessary device to secure the extra resources that schools must have if they are to respond appropriately to children's particular needs. However, I would suggest that the formal process of assessment and diagnosis *sometimes* serves the function of allowing parents and teachers, unconsciously, to distance themselves from the child's difficulty. Acquiring a Statement of Special Educational Need is complex and time-consuming and can be, in part, a distraction—an unconscious defence against the pain of engaging with the emotional experience.

This is, perhaps, particularly the case when the difficulty is primarily a behavioural one. I have written elsewhere (Youell, 1999b) about working with Educational and Behavioural Difficulties (EBD). I have suggested that these children are subject to a particular kind of hyperarousal and oversensitivity. Whether or not they have been traumatized by actual external events, children with EBD suffer from many of the symptoms of post-traumatic stress disorder. For these individuals, feeling states change at an alarming speed and the capacity to think and control their behaviour lags far behind. Things change internally very quickly and without warning, and this has a devastating effect on the way in which they can manage the external world.

In some instances, the label (e.g., ADHD, EBD) replaces some of the thinking that might usefully go on about the child's emotional experience, the nature of his relationships, and the nature of his internal world. Having a label or a diagnosis is sometimes confused with having a solution to the problem, as if knowing what is wrong automatically means knowing how to deal with it. It is very hard for those concerned with the child to stay with the worry and confusion, to pool ideas, and to tolerate not understanding for long enough to allow ideas to emerge. The availability of medication for children with ADHD is a very concrete example of this need for certainty, for a solution. There are all kinds of educational and behavioural programmes currently available that have been designed to meet the needs of particular groups of children. Many have been well researched and have much to offer. A well-constructed scheme of work, a behaviour-management programme, or proper use of medication can provide "containment" for teacher and pupil. However, much more important, in my view, is the containment that can be achieved in the relationships between teacher, learner, parent, and school institution when there is thoughtful exploration of unconscious as well as conscious communication.

CHAPTER NINE

Group dynamics in school

As human beings, we belong to groups that identify us, such as our gender or ethnicity. We belong to family units, and we are predisposed to seek out membership of other groups that help to define us and give meaning to our lives. Groups also challenge our capacity to cooperate with others, to be realistic about our own strengths and weaknesses, to recognize the contribution of others, and to tolerate difference.

A school institution is made up of a large number of groups, each with its own task and each with its own identity. Each group is connected in complicated ways to other groups and to the institution as a whole. Just as in society at large, some groups come together temporarily, some endure, some cluster informally around a shared experience or purpose, and some have formalized structures and rules governing membership and behaviour.

It is interesting to pause and think for a moment about how many groups the average adult human being belongs to in any one working day. A group of social workers on a course were asked to reflect on this, and one came up with the following list. She began, she said, as a member of her family, sharing a rather frantic breakfast time with children and partner. She walked her children round the corner to school, belonging briefly to a group of mothers at the school gate discussing a crisis over school lunches. On the tube train, she did not really think of her fellow passengers as a group, although there was a moment when the train stopped in a tunnel and several of them made eye contact, wordlessly sharing their anxiety. In her office, she sat at her desk among members of her area team before going to a Child Protection Case Conference, which brought together a range of professionals from several agencies for a formal meeting. After this, she went for a quick sandwich lunch with two colleagues and then to a team meeting. After the team meeting, she had supervision with her team leader and then went out on two home visits, spending about half an hour with each of two families. Back home, she prepared the children's supper before coming out to the course, and here she was, sitting among another group, her fellow students. Asked which experience had been the most problematic in terms of group dynamics, she quickly answered the Case Conference, with its diverse membership and difficult task. The team meeting came a close second!

A child's progress through a typical school day might be seen to be just as demanding in terms of group life, if not more so. A Year Five boy, for example, also starts his day by making the transition from family to school. In the playground, he waits with friends for the bell to ring and then lines up with his class group. After registration in his classroom, he goes to assembly, where he becomes part of the school as a whole, staff and children. Back in the classroom, the first half hour is spent in whole-class activity before dividing up into small groups to pursue particular tasks. Playtime arrives, and he plays football with a group of boys from Year Six until he is ejected in favour of one of their own peers. His class then join the other Year Five class for singing practice in the hall. Then he goes to the library with half of his class before going back to the classroom and from there to the dinner hall. He always shares a table with the same small group if possible, but today two teachers join them. In the afternoon there are science activities in small groups, before PE and then circle time with their class teacher and, lastly, story-time on the carpet with a classroom assistant. The after-school club sees him sitting with a group of children from various classes, trying to get his homework done so that there can be no argument about him going out to play with neighbourhood friends after tea.

To be able to manage such a complex series of group settings, the child needs to have a fairly robust sense of who he is, what contribution he can make, and what he has to learn from others. This is work that begins in the family group, according to Freud, the prototypical experience for all future group life. In the day described above, we see that the boy has to be able to move from small groups to large groups, from groups that are led by a teacher to groups that have no appointed leader; from groups that have a clearly defined task to groups that are little more than a random cluster of individuals. He spends time with his peers and, in the playground, briefly joins a group of older boys. He also has to manage the appearance and disappearance of adults: the staff in assembly, the teachers at the lunch table, the class teacher giving way to a classroom assistant at the very end of the afternoon. Some groups are based on age, some on gender, and some on factors such as whether or not children have to remain in after school club rather than going straight home. Relatively few groups in this child's day are based on recognition of particular abilities, although it is unlikely that poor players will be tolerated in the football game. It may also be that the teacher organizes the small-group tasks according to abilities and aptitudes, including aspects of personality as well as intellectual capacity.

The school is an institution, a large group, that comes together around the linked tasks of teaching and learning. As has been stressed in earlier chapters, learning and teaching inevitably involve anxiety. The psychoanalytic view of group membership is that it, too, involves anxiety. The school is then doubly challenged, being called on to manage a double dose of anxiety. If the challenge in providing learning opportunities is to keep the attendant anxiety within manageable bounds, so it is with group life. How can children be drawn into group life and be helped to manage their own anxiety and the complex, powerful dynamics of the group?

There is no denying the fact that many people, both children and adults, find groups very scary and will do their best to avoid them, particularly new groupings with new tasks to tackle. There are ways, in adult life, of reducing one's group participation while remaining within accepted social norms. Some people simply say that they are not sociable, that they "don't do" groups, teams, societies, and so on. Some choose to live in remote locations, to take up careers that focus on computers or machines rather than on human beings, and so forth. Some take their flight from the social world to extremes. I remember talking to a nun in an enclosed convent. She acknowledged that part of her motivation for taking her vows was to escape from social relationships. She laughed ironically as she said she had been foolish enough to imagine that relationships with her fellow nuns would be straightforward!

True social isolation can be a very dangerous thing. Many of the individuals who have committed serial murders or mass shootings in school or community settings have been described as "loners", "odd-balls", or "isolates". They have been living with only their own thoughts and feelings, their minds becoming pressure cookers without the pressure gauge and outlet that group life provides.

Hamish Canham (2002), writing about group and gang states of mind, points out that if the anxiety of group life can be harnessed, there is an unparalleled opportunity for growth and development. He suggests that there has been a tendency in psychoanalytic literature to focus on the destructive potential of collections of individuals, rather than on the creative potential of groups.

> What I have described are the more positive attributes of group life where projective processes are minimal, where there is a concern amongst members for each other ... where there remains a capacity to reflect and there is a predominantly benevolent atmosphere. It is these positive aspects of group life which give meaning and pleasure to being in a family or a work or friendship group and where the possibilities for creativity can surpass the capacities of any individual member. [p. 114]

Psychoanalytic theory and groups

Wilfred Bion's (1961) theories about group dynamics arose out of his experience as a psychoanalyst working with therapeutic

groups in post-war England. He was among the first to bring together psychoanalytic theory and group dynamics, and his ideas
have formed the basis for many developments and applications
over the past fifty years. Bion's vocabulary for thinking about
groups and institutions is still very much in currency and is as
relevant to schools as to any other setting.

Work groups and basic assumptions

Bion identified groups as a number of individuals coming together for a purpose: to "do" something. A group that is functioning well, which is on-task, he described as being in a "work-group"
state of mind and a group off-task as having allowed "basic assumption" behaviour to take hold. He thought about several kinds
of anti-task or basic assumption phenomena, each having its roots
in anxiety that cannot be contained (thought about) by the group
but is projected from group members into other group members.
The first basic assumption he suggested was dependence, with
members projecting all hope and competence into a leader, thereby
becoming passively dependent. The group no longer functions as
a group but as an unquestioning pack of followers. In the second
formulation, the group projects all it hopefulness into a pairing
that has taken place within its membership. This pair is seen as a
creative, sexual coupling, invested with the responsibility for Mes-
sianic rescue of the group. The third basic assumption is that of
fight or flight, where anxiety takes the group off-track and a leader
emerges to direct the fear or the fury towards a target that has little
to do with the agreed task of the group.

Another way to think about this would be to suggest that a
group in "work-group" mode is demonstrating depressive-position characteristics, whereas the "basic assumption" behaviour is
more akin to the paranoid-schizoid position, where splitting and
projection predominate (chapter 2).

Valency

Bion (1961) defines valency as being the individual's readiness
to take on a role or play a part for the group in its basic assumption

behaviour. He suggests that everyone has a valency of one kind or another, that to be free of valency is not a possibility if one is to remain human and in contact with other humans.

To give a more workaday description of what we mean by valency would be to say that it describes something of what we, as individuals, bring to groups—our unconscious contribution to the dynamics. Most of us have had the experience of finding ourselves in a group situation, behaving in a way that feels out of character and was certainly not intended. We may be shocked that we could have become so angry, so upset, so determined, so competitive, or whatever. We may find ourselves being unusually loud or quiet, provocative or conciliatory. In social groupings we may be suddenly flirtatious and reckless or cautious and disapproving. If these responses are truly out of character, it is probably the case that we have been the recipients of powerful projections of parts of the personalities of other group members. They have sat back and watched us "make a fool of ourselves", or so it feels. In any group, there are, as it were, parts waiting for actors to take them up. However, if a pattern emerges and we find that we are always being blown off task in a particular way, playing a particular role in the group, then it is likely that we have discovered something about our valency for being the recipient of particular kinds of projections. Recognizing our own valency, or that of our pupils or colleagues, is to bring it into the conscious domain, to make it available for thought—the first step in being able to alter our own behaviour or influence the behaviour of others in a group setting.

How useful is Bion's formulation to thinking about the behaviour of groups in classrooms and staffrooms? With the addition of a few concepts, it provides, in my view, an invaluable tool for the teacher, who is able to achieve an observational stance in relation to her own behaviour and that of her pupils and colleagues. Very few groups manage to remain in "work-group" mode for any length of time, but observation of the interactions may enable the individual (whether or not a participant) to identify something of the origins of the basic assumption behaviour, to recognize the valencies of group members, and occasionally to make an intervention to bring the group back on task.

Rules

One way in which groups seek to avoid unexpected or unmanageable expressions of feeling is by establishing rules and regulations. ·

Committees have a Chair, a Secretary, and an Agenda in an attempt to keep the group on task and within the agreed time boundary. "Any other business" is tagged on to the formal agenda to reassure members that they have an opportunity to raise their particular concerns or to make an impact on the meeting. It allows for a small amount of spontaneity in what is otherwise a somewhat circumscribed group event. However, we have all been at meetings where time boundaries slip, where the Chair loses control of the Agenda, where one or more group members "hog the floor", and where decisions are never reached. The conventions of meetings of this kind provide a framework for the group; they do not inoculate the group against the impact of unconscious processes. Any or all of the basic assumption behaviours can take hold of a committee and lead it off-task.

The same is true of even the most rule-bound of activities. A group of people getting together to play a game, whether it be tennis or Monopoly, have agreed to abide by a set of rules. However, as somebody begins to win and somebody else drops behind, feelings get stirred up and all kinds of behaviour may erupt. Activities that are explicitly competitive demand that group members manage feelings about winning and losing, that they are not too triumphant in victory, and that they accept failure without accusing anybody of cheating, without blaming their partner, and so on.

By contrast, a group of close friends sharing a casual drink in the pub may have unspoken rules about taking turns to buy a round, but otherwise the structure is loose and the membership of the group is fluid. The agenda is not fixed, and so the conversation could go in any direction and could run into areas of conflict, stirring up unconscious dynamics. On the other hand, the task of the group is relatively unchallenging (to have a drink together), there is little pressure, and so anxiety may be at a minimum. Formalized rules are not needed.

Schools and classrooms need rules in order to function. As soon as children arrive in school, they are introduced to the basic rules of school life. These include rules that, it is hoped, have been established in the family (e.g., no hurting each other) as well as some that are specific to the school or the classroom. Teachers impose all kinds of rules that enable them to manage large numbers of children, large amounts of equipment, and the demands of the curriculum. These rules are designed to enable the children to live in close proximity with each other as well as to be able to learn, and it is vitally important that children have the security that a sensible set of rules provides. However, the imposition of rules in the classroom cannot provide complete protection from the impact of unconscious group processes. I think this is now fully accepted in schools where self-reflective practice is the norm. I think it was not so in the schools of the past, where fear of disruption led teachers and head teachers to impose more and more rules, accompanied by more and more severe sanctions. Indeed, I may be being overly optimistic in thinking that things are fundamentally different now. Government still tends to respond defensively to challenges to the social order, whether in schools or elsewhere, imposing harsher penalties rather than stopping to reflect on possible causes of the disruption.

Paranoid rules

Some institutions, clubs, and societies protect their boundaries and territory with elaborate entry requirements and codes of behaviour. These are usually designed to keep out undesirable influences and to maintain a uniformity or sameness about the group. This kind of paranoid organization is based on fear of difference and diversity. The members of the group, in theory, are protected from having to deal with questions about their own shortcomings; these can all be projected outside the club, into those who are excluded from membership. Those outside the group then carry all the unwanted aspects of the personality and, in phantasy, become even more frightening and threatening, so that the club has to reinforce its barriers to make sure that they never find a way in. In thinking about examples of this kind of group, one's mind naturally goes to social-class divisions and to some of the "exclusive" gentlemen's clubs of the West End of London, some golf clubs, tennis clubs, and so on, as well as to the Working Men's Clubs in the north of England and the Miner's Guilds in South Wales. However, the description applies just as accurately to clubs that are defined along different lines—clubs that effectively restrict their membership to people of a particular political persuasion, to particular racial groups, to women, to male homosexuals, and so on. We now have "gated communities" which keep out those who cannot afford to buy their way in and which protect themselves from intruders with locks and alarms. We also have run-down estates that are "out of bounds" to anybody who does not live there.

Canham (2002) suggests that groups that rely on sameness are likely to stagnate in their own narcissism: "A group which always agrees with itself and cannot bear dissent or conflict is doomed to omnipotence, complacency and smugness" (p. 114).

At their very worst, some of the selective schools of the 1950s might have been accused of something of this kind of paranoid outlook. The dismantling of the grammar school system in the 1970s and subsequent reforms have done much to eradicate formalized "exclusivity" in the education system. "Inclusion" is now the watchword, and most schools are genuinely diverse, multicultural, multiethnic, mixed-ability institutions. Again, this does not mean that schools are immune from paranoid thinking or that groups within schools do not manage to get themselves into this kind of state of mind, where all the energy and focus is on perpetuating sameness and resisting innovation. It is also worth noting that there is currently a move back to separation of school populations through innovations such as City Academies, or Centres of Excellence, as well as the proliferation of single-faith schools.

Scapegoating

Groups of all kinds, but perhaps particularly in schools and colleges, are inclined to target projections at a particular recipient, who becomes a scapegoat for all the group's ills. This individual is identified with failure and may become an intolerable presence in the group, reminding the other group members both of their own shortcomings and their culpability in treating one of their members so badly. The greater the stress and pressure the group is under, the more likely it is that a scapegoat will be found. At times of inspection, for example, there may be a groundswell of opinion that a particular pupil must be excluded. If an inspection goes badly, there may be an uprising against one teacher or manager, who is seen as responsible for the failure.

Scapegoating takes place in the day-to-day life of most groups. Even if the identified scapegoat is not actually ejected from the group, he or she will be made to feel that he or she is dragging the group down and has ruined the group's chances of success.

Some years ago, when working as a peripatetic behaviour support teacher, I was asked to do some observations of the "sink" Year Nine class (9W) in a run-down inner-city secondary school. The head of year told me that it would be very helpful if I could identify the ringleaders so that they could be removed from the school. He was sick of everybody complaining that the class was unteachable. He had tried temporary exclusions, but nothing had improved. I spent two days shadowing the class and watching the way in which they fell into line with what was now expected of them. Teachers arrived late to teach their lessons, their books were not marked, and, almost invariably, somebody was immediately sent to the head of year for some infringement of a uniform rule or for chewing gum. No attempt was made to intervene when the young people spread themselves around the benches in the science lab in a way that was bound to lead to trouble. The science teacher tried to ignore everything that was going on beyond the first bench, which was populated by a small group of girls who pronounced themselves eager to do the lesson. When a riot broke out at the back of the room and the teacher went to intervene, this group packed up their bags and took out fashion magazines.

The one exception to this pattern was form time. Form 9W's teacher was not going to give up on them. She worked hard to establish a friendly relationship with each and every one of them and was very pleased to have me join her in thinking about them. It was clear to us that this class was something of a scapegoat for the school as a whole and that to identify one or more children for expulsion was no solution. We agreed that it would be more productive to see if we could find a way to get the class to function better as a group and to persuade the school (the staff) to take back some of the projections with which the class was burdened.

With the help of the form teacher, I divided the class into four groups, mixed in terms of ability, gender, and race. This inevitably meant that friendship groups were split up, although I tried to ensure that everybody would be able to identify with at least one other member of their group. Each group had four group meetings over a four-week period. I had to work out a complicated timetable to ensure that they did not always miss the same lesson. To my amazement, they managed to follow the timetable and, after the first week, turned up to their session with a reasonable degree of enthusiasm. I did not do anything very ambitious. We played some word games and drama games (requiring them to think about how they would describe themselves and each other), and we played board games for the last fifteen minutes of each session. They sometimes had to play with somebody they did not know, and boys had to play with girls. We spent one session on what they thought of their class (9W), and it became clear that they had taken in the school's view. It was painful to hear them describe their class as "really bad", "thick", "stupid", "rubbish". This was in marked contrast to what they said about each other as individuals, and this discrepancy did not escape their notice.

The head of year and head teacher had been very sceptical about my plan and, when I offered feedback, were still asking me to identify the key troublemakers. However, the feedback session with all the teachers who taught the class went much better. I gave them time to express their despair and agreed that the class was difficult, acknowledging that I had only had to cope with seven at a time and it had not always been easy. They, like the children, began to identify areas of commonality and areas of difference in their experience, and by the end of the meeting there was a livelier atmosphere in the room.

Some weeks later, I enquired of the head teacher as to how 9W was faring, only to be told that they were fine—9Z was now the problem! My understanding of this was not that there had been a total transformation but, rather, that 9W and their teachers were managing to avoid or reject some of the projected feelings of failure, and the focus had therefore shifted onto 9Z.

Group work in schools

Recent years have seen a proliferation of group-work interventions in schools. Groups of children, young people, or, indeed, parents are invited to come together to talk about issues of common interest or concern. Some are managed by the schools themselves, others are facilitated by professionals from outside the school. All have the common aim of improving understanding and improving the quality of group life. "Circle time" is now a standard part of personal and social education in primary schools, with class teachers presiding over frank discussions about social and emotional experience. Children are encouraged in the safety of the group to speak about their own feelings and thoughts and to listen respectfully to what others have to say. They are also encouraged to imagine what might be the experience of other children whose lives are very different from their own. They are encouraged to voice their thoughts about each other's behaviour and to think about issues such as classroom disruption. This kind of structured group activity does much to validate emotional experience and establish a culture of openness. When managed well, this is a creative experience for the group and for the individual pupil. When managed badly, I fear it can lead to splits, with some children occupying the moral high ground, projecting their unwanted parts into others.

Group size

There is most certainly an optimum group size for any given task. Take, for example, a task such as organizing the equipment in the classroom, including making a rota for using the computers.

A group of five 11-year-olds should be able to tackle the task fairly quickly and efficiently, so long as they are motivated to do so and do not get caught up in disagreements about who should take the lead. A group of fifteen would find the same task much more difficult. They would be likely to find themselves arguing as to how to start, as to who should lead the project, as to whose ideas should be adopted, and so on. They might even splinter into smaller groups, with everyone wanting to feel that they had a key role. Alternatively, a sub-group might get on with the task while other group members opted out, drifting off to do other things. A group of thirty children would be unlikely to get past square one.

Teaching large numbers is challenging. However, there is a common misconception in schools that teaching small groups is easy. Children with learning difficulties or challenging behaviour are often removed from the large-group setting in the classroom to work in a small group. Teachers, support assistants, and mentors who do this kind of work often do not want to admit that they find it difficult. After all, they should be able to cope with just three children when the class teacher has the other twenty-seven! What is not always taken into account is the inbuilt difficulty for some children of managing in a family-sized group. The group experience resonates with family life and stirs up feelings of jealousy and rivalry. The children compete for the attention and approval of the one teacher, the parent in the transference. The internal/ unconscious preoccupations of the individual children come to the surface and produce a heady cocktail of passionate love and hatred. The most difficult teaching experience I can remember was in a psychiatric unit where I was one of two teachers working with a small group of young adolescents. At first, we could not understand why it was easier to teach the group of six than it was to have just two boys in the classroom. We eventually realized that when it was just the two of us and the two of them, we turned into a parental couple in the transference. Individually they competed for our attention, together they sought to undermine our authority, punish us for our failures, and make sure that nothing creative could happen between us. It was a salutary lesson, and one that has remained with me. Some children need a high adult-to-child ratio and may need a certain amount of one-to-one attention, but they do not necessarily benefit from being placed with one adult and a small number of peers.

Group dynamics in the staffroom

The situation for teachers in the staffroom is different only in that there is an expectation that, as adults, they know themselves better and have more capacity to stay in touch with thinking. There is an expectation that depressive-position functioning will predominate and that paranoid-schizoid behaviour will only occur under great pressure. This may be so, but it has to recognized that groups amplify whatever anxiety is around, and in group situations everyone is vulnerable to basic assumption behaviour.

Job descriptions and person specifications for teaching posts now make reference to "the ability to work as a member of a team" as standard. Every teacher is part of a staff group as a whole but will also be a member of a particular year-group team, a special-needs team, a senior-management team, a specialist-subject team, and possibly more than one of these groupings. Each sub-group of this kind has a hierarchy, as does the school as a whole. There are formal differences of status, salary, and responsibility, as well as informal ones in terms of differences in perceived competence as a teacher and popularity with pupils. There are also immense pressures coming in from outside the school—from parents, from the local authority, from central government. Head teachers have to run a business as well as a community, and the interests of the two do not always tally. In short, there is every reason for anxiety to take hold of groups, with splitting, projection, and scapegoating becoming rife.

CHAPTER TEN

Projective processes:
gangs, bullying, and racism

Groups and gangs

When does a group become a gang? Hamish Canham (2002) defines a gang mentality as one in which destructive forces have taken over. It is paranoid-schizoid functioning where there is no thinking, only a need to rid oneself of parts of the personality that might expose the individual (or group) to feelings of neediness, ignorance, or weakness. Within the personality, this is achieved by imposing a reign of terror on the vulnerable parts. In gang behaviour, the reign of terror is directed towards other groups. A gang is anti-thought, anti-parents, and anti-life.

Hamish offers a commentary on William Golding's *The Lord of the Flies* and tracks the way in which the boys lose touch with an idea of parental function and give way to the lure of the gang. He draws attention to the way in which Ralph and Piggy manage to impose some structure by making the rule about the conch: in community meetings, boys cannot speak unless they are holding the conch. At the beginning of their time on the island, the older boys are in touch with the idea of rules (which Hamish suggests are a representation of parental function), and they agree to this arrangement. Later, the rule is cast aside, the conch smashed, and order is overthrown in an outpouring of paranoid-schizoid behaviour.

Jack, the leader of the choir, represents the pull in the group away from feeling lonely, afraid and dependent on each other for survival. The de-personalisation that sets in is represented by the dyes with which these boys begin to daub their faces. Jack, in particular, is gripped by an idée fixe which is that their survival is dependent on killing the pigs which inhabit the jungle interior of the island. This culminates in a horrific scene where a sow with a litter of suckling piglets is killed by Jack and his band of followers.

This action represents most dramatically the gang mentality at work. Faced with a life without parents to look after them, vulnerability and loss is projected into the pig family, with the piglets made into the orphans the boys feel themselves to be. As those who have read the novel will know, this cruelty extends to brutal savagery from Jack and his gang towards the other boys, in particular Piggy, who is killed towards the end of the book.

Piggy is an overweight, asthmatic boy who has an ability to see the truth of their situation and to continue thinking about what needs to be done to ensure the survival of everyone. Piggy's thoughtfulness and insight is under constant attack from the gang. They steal his glasses—representing his capacity to see—and eventually they kill him. Ralph is the character who struggles most between the lure of the gang and his desire not to lose the capacity to think. As he is pulled towards the gang, Golding describes a shutter coming down in Ralph's mind. This shutter seems to cut him off from what he knows he should be doing—keeping the fire going, looking after the younger children, building shelters and keeping everyone working together. It represents the temptation for him to forget these responsibilities and to join Jack's gang who seem to be leading a life free from these worries as they hunt for pigs.

It is most striking that the only two characters in the book who make reference to their families in any significant way are Piggy and Ralph. It seems that it is this ability to keep alive a sense of helpful, loving parental figures that sustains these two boys and helps them not to climb into identification with the parodies of powerful grown-ups as Jack and his followers do. [pp. 119–120]

Children and young students in schools are not faced with this kind of ordeal, involving total separation from adult control and protection. However, there may be times when the experience of groups or individuals will have some elements in common with what is described in the novel, and their emotional responses may be similar.

Hamish Canham summarizes what can be seen as the teacher's (or school institution's) role as follows:

> The presence of figures in authority who can maintain a thoughtful and considerate attitude towards all those for whom they have responsibility inclines people towards groupings rather than "ganging". This may be within a family, the classroom, work place or in government. The presence of these figures is, of course, not sufficient in itself, for they will be distorted by the perceptions of those reliant on them. This relationship is crucial and is centrally determined by the results of working through the Oedipus complex in individuals. [p. 125]

The internal world and the gang state of mind

This brings us back to the question of what is going on in the internal worlds of children and young people who, as Hamish suggests, distort their perception of external reality such that they cannot make use of thoughtful, concerned adults. He writes about a "ganging" within the mind, which drives children towards gangs in the external world or turns them into nasty, scheming bullies. "The dominant and destructive parts of the self take hostage what they feel to be those other parts which would expose them to feelings of neediness, littleness and ignorance and they do so by imposing a reign of terror on those other parts." In this state of mind, the individual is clinging to the illusion of omnipotence and omniscience; there is no separation from the object and no acknowledgement of dependency. The parent in the internal world is a nasty, narcissistic version, seeking only to rid him/herself of any awareness of vulnerability or need for others.

Bullies and victims

The bullies of school stories (e.g., Flashman in *Tom Brown's School-days*, Squeers in *Nicholas Nickelby*) fit neatly into this psychological account of extreme splitting and projection. They are unrelenting in their attacks on their victims and continue with their escalating cruelty until such time as they get their just deserts. Most of the time, the situation is much less polarized. If paranoid-schizoid functioning and the depressive position are seen as states of mind between which all human beings oscillate, then it follows that everyone is capable of bullying behaviour of one kind or another. When interviewed sensitively and encouraged to be honest, most children admit to having at one time or another bullied a weaker member of the class, a younger sibling, or an animal. Most children can also describe interactions or relationships in which they have been the victims of bullying. They are also able to speak eloquently about how they understand the motivation behind bullying, seeing very clearly that the bully is trying to get rid of feelings he does not want to have.

The cliché about there being a coward inside every bully is, of course, accurate. However, a psychoanalytic account would suggest that the perceived threat comes as much from within the individual as from the external world. If, after an episode of bullying behaviour, the individual is able to get back in touch with good internal objects and associated depressive functioning, he will be able to think about his own culpability and to feel some remorse. If this is not possible, the bully is indeed in a terrifying world, one in which his hostile projections lodge in objects which then become all the more toxic and threatening, as the fear of retaliation increases. When bullying becomes entrenched, the bully has to redouble his efforts to make sure that there is no chink in his armour. Part of this is likely to be to surround himself with a gang—a group of followers who have their own reasons for sticking close to the bully. The leader of the gang works hard to make sure that everybody knows it would be dangerous to leave—a clear projection of his own knowledge that he would be in danger without them. This is the theme of many books and films as well as the school stories mentioned above. The Mafia, for example, is not an organization that people choose to leave or, indeed, where there is room for independent thought!

Origins of the gang state of mind

In terms of child development and early experience, the lamentable internal situation of the hardened bully or gang member may come about in a number of ways. Hamish Canham (2002) draws attention to the kinds of experiences that, in his view, may create the "gang state of mind". He refers to the impact of extreme anxiety and the tendency in human beings to look for someone to blame. He also identifies deprivation in terms of a deficit in containment in early life, which he suggests renders the individual less able to hold on to depressive position functioning and more likely to resort to projection and splitting. He writes about the impact of abuse and the way in which children who have been the victims of abusive treatment often seek to rid themselves of the feelings of fear, anger, guilt, and shame by passing on the experience, by vacating the position of victim and putting another in their place.

CASE ILLUSTRATION: ROBERT

Robert was a bully. At 10 years of age, he had a reputation in his school for terrorizing anyone who was smaller or weaker than he was. His teachers knew what he got up to but could rarely catch him at it. If they did see him, for example, leaning over a younger child against a wall in a corner of the playground, they would try to intervene, but he would quickly put a positive spin on what he was doing and his hapless victim would corroborate his story. He was usually flanked on either side by boys of physical bulk and low intelligence. They considered themselves to be highly privileged to have been singled out by him, and if they ever felt a tinge of discomfort about what they were seeing, they were very quickly pulled back into line.

Robert seemed entirely comfortable in his position as leader of his gang. Without actually causing physical hurt, he managed to provide himself and his followers with extra money, extra food, the best seats in the dining hall, and first turn on the football pitch. He was intimidating. He was also capable of making his own classmates fall about with laughter, and they looked on with some satisfaction as he tried out a bit of mockery (verbal bullying) of an inexperienced supply teacher.

Shortly before he was due to visit possible schools in advance of secondary transfer, he was accused of going into the girls' toilets and of looking up the girls' skirts. A 9-year-old girl had been upset at home, and her parents came into the school to complain. The head teacher subsequently spoke to Robert, who first denied it and then broke down and begged him not to tell his father. The next day, having received a call from the head and a letter giving the reasons for a three-day exclusion, Robert's father stormed into school. He barged past the receptionist and straight into the head teacher's room, demanding an explanation. Towering over the head's desk, he shouted that his boy was innocent and that it was just typical of this school to pick on an innocent child. He thumped the desk as he said that if there was any more trouble of this kind, he would make life miserable for the head, adding that he did not need anyone to tell him how to bring up his child. If there was any punishment to be meted out, he would do it himself.

A very much cowed Robert returned to school three days later. The head spoke to him immediately and suggested he see the school counsellor. The counsellor continued to see him until he moved on to secondary school. Sessions were filled with a great deal of empty bravado, but Robert did manage to talk more honestly as the relationship developed, and his bullying behaviour diminished over the last few months of his primary school career. The counsellor came to understand that Robert was terrified of growing up. He had very little internal sense of supportive adults who would help him to do so. He was sure that he would be bullied in secondary school and that his father would mock him for it. He was already mocked by his older brothers for not being more sexually advanced, hence his exploit in the girls' toilets. He had no confidence in his academic ability and so believed that physical strength was his only way of staying "ahead of the game". Being "ahead of the game" seemed to be his version of being able to survive—physically, emotionally, and psychologically. The counsellor was convinced that Robert was treated harshly at home, but he was fiercely loyal to his father and would not give anything away about his home life.

The way in which Robert fits in with Hamish Canham's description of the development of a gang state of mind is clear. At 10 years old, he has a model in his mind which is of needing to make himself feel better by making others feel worse. He surrounds himself with supporters and provides himself with stolen goods to boost his flagging self-esteem. He cannot dwell on his fears for the future and is heavily identified with his bullying father. Mockery threatens him from without and from within. It is a hopeful sign that his counsellor managed to make some contact with a more vulnerable and honest aspect of Robert, and one would want to think that a similar resource would be made available for him in secondary school. The onset of puberty, with all the associated physical, psychological, and emotional changes, could so easily throw him back into an identification with a gang leader.

Envy and the bully

I want to broaden the discussion about deprivation in the internal world and make some links with deprivation in the external world and with the destructive forces of envy. It is absolutely clear that poverty does not, of itself, breed destructive envy. If there is a secure internal structure based on experiences of containment and of having been helped to negotiate separation, the materially impoverished individual is unlikely to be consumed by envy of his richer neighbour. However, where internal deprivation of the kind Hamish describes meets external deprivation, there is fertile ground for envy and hatred. Poverty and deprivation may then be used by individuals to justify their membership of gangs which, they argue, only exist to right the perceived injustice. This is a particular danger when the impoverished individual is constantly brought up against the affluence of others. There have been major changes in this aspect of the external-world context since the early psychoanalytic theorists were struggling to reach an understanding of projective processes. This kind of provocation—the provocation of relative wealth—can be seen in inner cities, where rich and poor communities live side by side. It can also be seen in communities where there is widespread poverty and despair but where satellite television suggests that there is a shiny, exciting world just out of reach. Envy of what others seem to have acquired without effort is one of the major determinants of the gang state of mind. Globalization, advertising, ideas of instant wealth and fame, and the preoccupation with celebrity all serve to challenge the sense of identity of the individual, and particularly so if feelings of relative poverty resonate with an internal picture that is full of deprivation.

Racism

Bullying and racism are different in some important detail but also have much in common with each other. I do not intend to suggest that a psychological account of racism can replace a sociological or political account. As Stephen Frosh (1989) suggests, racism, like sexism, is deeply embedded in Western society, having its external, historical roots in economic and political oppression. However, the question to be addressed is whether a psychological understanding of the internal dynamics of racism can contribute anything of value to those who are charged with responsibility for managing the issue in our schools. Frosh makes the point that it is the racist fear and hatred in the psyche of individuals that perpetuates institutionalized racism.

This is a debate that is often felt to be too risky to address. Our language in health, education, and social care is peppered with phrases that are designed to make everyone feel more comfortable—"working with difference", "anti-discriminatory practice", "cultural sensitivity", and so on. These may be worthy aims, but they all too easily serve to inhibit thought, in that they sanitize and oversimplify an area of discourse that is rife with passionate feelings of love, hatred, and fear. I want to be clear that I am not dodging the question of how schools can make a contribution to the anti-racist cause, but, rather, arguing that enhanced understanding of the mechanism within individuals must surely make a contribution to thinking about the curriculum and about whole-school policies.

The racist individual

On an individual level, racism is another manifestation of projective processes. The racist targets a particular individual or an ethnic group, who become the recipients of a cluster of hostile projections. Thoughts and feelings that the individual does not want to own get attached to a racial identity. That race is then hated because of the characteristics that have been attributed to it and feared because there is an unconscious expectation that there will be retaliation. The racist has to ensure that he is justified in his hatred, and this he does—in a similar way to the bully—by gathering like-minded supporters around him and by justifying his position with arguments about the way in which the hated race has brought it on itself. Economic realities such as pressure on housing or benefits are brought into the argument in the service of bolstering a system that is actually about generating paranoid fear and hatred in an attempt to manage internal anxiety. Envy fuels the racism when the racist thinks he sees the hated group succeeding where he feels himself to be failing.

Fear of difference and change

It is easy to write or speak about "the racist". It is much more difficult to address aspects of fear, prejudice, and intolerance in ourselves. In the chapter on beginnings and endings (chapter 6), I have written about the tendency in the human psyche to try to hold onto the status quo, actively resisting forces that challenge our assumptions and threaten our equilibrium. "Working with difference" and "celebrating diversity" suddenly become much more challenging notions if we are genuinely open to new experience and really allow for the fact that we might need to change our perspective and that change involves discomfort.

For my own generation, growing up in the 1950s and early 1960s, ignorance was a major part of the picture. The idea of "The

Commonwealth" was a comfortable cocoon in which to hide from the realities of inequality, exploitation, and oppression. Childhood songs, rhymes, and stories were racist in content, but we did not know it (consciously) and were not called upon to be ashamed of reciting them. Things have moved on since then, and children now have the benefit of a more rounded version of history and first-hand knowledge of other ethnic groups and other cultures. Schools have played a vital role in educating children over several generations about each other's histories and cultural identities, and this has done much to eradicate some of the stereotyping and racist assumptions which, historically, were based on ignorance.

The situation in the early twenty-first century is very different. Mass migration has continued to grow over the past fifty years, and we now live in much more mixed communities. We are also subject to the inexorable impact of world news and commentary. Social divisions are now racialized in a way that can all too readily be used to legitimize the words or behaviour of the racist individual.

Cooper and Lousada (2005) make some interesting points in a paper that they call "The Psychic Geography of Racism". They suggest that in the last decade or more, there has been a loss of the "believed-in family", by which they mean that there has been a change in the relationship between citizen and state. "Upon the quality of the relationship between citizen and state depends the depth or shallowness of social concern" (p. 86). They suggest that in the past there was a relationship with an idea of the "Welfare State", which was built on assumptions of benign leadership where government and those in positions of authority would concern themselves with the needs of all those for whom they have responsibility. The population now knows much more about the actual people and institutions who are invested with these responsibilities and so has developed a much more cynical attitude.

Cooper and Lousada's thesis is that with the loss of the "believed-in family" comes the loss of a capacity for concern for the stranger. Acceptance of the stranger gives way to fear of the stranger and the growth of "nationalism, racial and social indifference". Schools reflect the society they serve, and I would suggest that there is something one might call the "believed-in" school institution where there is sufficient containment from the senior management team for tolerance and concern to hold sway. If the "believed-in" school is undermined, there is fertile ground for projective processes (ganging, bullying, and racism) to take hold.

Whole-school policies

Anti-racist and anti-bullying policy statements are important documents that give a clear message to staff, pupils, and parents as to what is and is not acceptable in school. Many local authorities now require that any incidence of bullying or racist behaviour be recorded. The record becomes part of the annual report from each school and, in that sense, is a public document. A thoughtfully constructed policy can be a genuine indication that a school is aiming to offer a "believed-in-family" context for learning and teaching. It can also, in some instances, be used defensively, as if the existence of a statement can in some way guarantee a tolerant and inclusive institution. Children and teachers should, of course, be prevented from speaking or behaving in a racist way. The curriculum should, of course, be genuinely multicultural, reflecting the experience of every member of the school community. All this is part of thoughtful and containing (Bion, 1961) management of the institution.

However, prejudice cannot be managed didactically. Teaching tolerance and understanding is a much more complicated task. There is a danger that Personal and Social Education (PSE) becomes infected by unconscious anxiety and unwittingly settles for teaching "about" diversity, never finding a safe way to explore some of the more primitive fears and feelings that groups have about difference. There is also a danger that the teaching takes up a rather comfortable "us" and "them" position, encouraging "us" to make space for "them" (the newcomers) and not addressing the nature of the minority experience and the feelings "they" have about "us". In my view, the very use of the word "minority" highlights one of the most powerful unconscious forces: the need to reassure oneself that one is in the "majority".

A major challenge of the early twenty-first century is how to understand the way in which international and inter-communal hatred has resulted in barbaric acts of terrorism in so many parts of the world. What is it that drives a young man to sacrifice his own life in order to take the lives of others in the name of nation, race, or religion, and what impact does this have on the polarization of religious and political factions? At the time of writing, the response of the UK government to the London bombings of 2005 has been to introduce legislation to prosecute those who incite hatred. Again, we see a device to control behaviour, which may be necessary but which seems to be entirely split off from thinking about the underlying issues.

These are huge questions, and we do not currently know how events will unfold, but there is a very simple point to be made about the importance of education and the vital role of schools. We neglect issues of racial, cultural, and religious identity at our peril, and it may be that combining a psychological account with a socio-political account in relation to human development and school communities would provide us with new and energizing perspectives.

CHAPTER ELEVEN

Families and schools

The family as a group

The family is the first group the child belongs to. It is the arrival of a baby which transforms a couple into a family unit, establishing a new generation in the extended family group. It is in this context that the child does much of his important growing up, and it is here that the building blocks of future learning and development are established. Indeed, the psychoanalytic view of families and group behaviour is that the emotional experiences in the mother–father–baby triangle are the ones that shape the personality and are carried forward into later group experience. The family is the launch pad for future relationships.

There is now an enormous range of family patterns, due to social changes such as the increase in divorce rate, the proliferation of temporary partnerships, gay parenthood, and so on. I need to be clear at the outset that lone-parent families are not excluded from the model of couple and child forming a nuclear unit. The baby of a lone mother has a father, even if unidentified, and the family triangle of mother, father, and baby is made up by the father figure whom the mother and baby have in their minds. There is also very likely to be a significant adult in the external world (friend or relative) who supports the mother (or lone father) and provides the third perspective, the third angle of the triangle.

The nuclear family

The impact of the arrival of a baby into a couple's lives is incalculable. However planned, wanted, and prepared for, the first baby disturbs the status quo in a fundamental way. Both parents are likely to be put in touch with aspects of their own infancies and may find themselves feeling strangely raw and emotionally labile. Along with the joy and sense of achievement comes the anxiety of suddenly being responsible for a dependent, vulnerable human being. The couple have to come to terms with the inevitable changes to their own relationship. Any description of this kind necessarily involves making generalizations, but each of the following generalizations is borne out by observation and by what young couples have reported. New mothers are usually absorbed in their babies in a way that fathers cannot fully share. Fathers often feel excluded from the intimacy of the mother–baby couple, and this is sometimes experienced as having been actively ejected, supplanted in the mother's affections by the baby. One young father was deeply shocked when he forgot the existence of his baby, leaving him in the back of the car for a few minutes before realizing there was something amiss! Another acknowledged that his unconscious ambivalence went one stage further when he forgot he was married and went out for a drink after work, leaving wife and baby at home, wondering what had happened to him.

After the first phase of immersion in the baby, mothers begin to look around and may feel that their partners have lost interest in them and fear that they won't be able to regain the earlier relationship. They may begin to feel trapped at home with the baby while the father has all the life in the outside world, with work and potential new relationships. Early return to work for mothers may be an economic necessity, but it may also be a response to feeling that aspects of their identity are threatened by the demands of motherhood. Fathers may also begin to feel restricted by the demands of the family and long for free evenings or weekends. With ambivalence comes guilt and sometimes mutual recrimination.

From the baby's perspective, the experience is one of having to come to terms with the fact that he does not have all of his mother all of the time, that there is another adult who has a claim to her, and that he sometimes has to wait. Awareness that these two adults have a relationship that is independent of him brings the oedipal situation into focus and stirs up hostile feelings and phantasies. In short, the nuclear family is rife with ambivalence—with envy, jealousy, rivalry, and hatred, as well as profound feelings of love and commitment.

Ron Britton (1989) writes about the oedipal situation in terms of a triangular space created by mother, father, and baby, within which emotional experience can be thought about and managed. The creation of this space within the triangle depends on the relationships being genuinely triangular, with three different and separate twosomes functioning within the safety of the threesome. This idea of a reflective space would seem to be the prototype for what Meltzer and Harris (1986) describe as the *introjective* function of the family unit. Their formulation is that the family's task is to promulgate love and hope, to contain pain, and to promote thinking. The family must also protect children from harm, introduce them to the social world, and promote their growth, with a view to their eventual separation.

I hope that the following extract from a family observation will serve to illustrate some of these ideas.

Monica (mother) opened the front door and told me that they were in the front room. As we entered the sitting-room, I saw that 7-month-old Georgie was sitting in the middle of the floor in front, on his play-mat, his back supported by a wall of cushions. In front of him was a large, colourful abacus toy and around his feet a few other favourite toys. He did not look around at first, absorbed as he was in reaching for one of the brightly coloured beads on the abacus. I was talking to his mother, and it was not until she spoke that he turned his head and gave her a huge smile. She pointed out that I had arrived, and I greeted him as I sat down. He stared at me with some caution in his look, but his mother reminded him who I was and clearly was herself untroubled by my presence. Reassured that I was a welcome guest, his face relaxed and he turned back to his play. We discussed the merits of the various toys, and his mother showed me the way a battery-operated train trundled along the carpet, making cheerful noises. She said that she thought it was wonderful and made it run again. Georgie giggled and bounced up and down, clapping his hands together in delight.

Georgie's father arrived with cups of tea and sat down. Both parents engaged me in conversation, but, every now and then, all our attention would turn to the baby and one or other parent would get down on the floor to point something out to him or bring something within his reach. He always rewarded them with a smile, and they spoke to me about how completely charming he is at the moment and how much they enjoy playing with him. When his father, who was sitting behind him, broke into full-hearted laughter, Georgie copied; he turned to his father and laughed in exactly the same way—as if joining in the joke. He twisted right round and toppled forward and then, finding himself on his front, tried to crawl towards his father.

As my visit went on, Georgie began to grizzle. His father picked him up, commenting on his feeling left out, and offered him a cuddle. After a few minutes on his father's lap, he was ready to go back on the floor and focus on a toy again.

The doorbell heralded the noisy arrival of his 6-year-old sister, Holly, back from a Halloween party. Georgie greeted her with a smile, but she stopped in her tracks at the door of the sitting-room and looked cross, as if to say "What's going on here without me? What have I missed?" She did not say this but addressed me somewhat aggressively: "I didn't know you were coming!" Her mother exclaimed at this impolite greeting, and Holly looked a little shamefaced. She glared at her baby brother on his hearthrug throne, pushed past him, disturbing the cushions, and threw herself into her father's arms. Her mother said something about changing out of her party dress, and Holly protested that it was not fair; they had said she could go "trick-or-treating" to Adam's house. Her mother responded that it was too late and Georgie needed his supper and so did she. Holly again cast her brother a hostile glance, before turning to her father to beg to go to Adam's house ... just for a few minutes. Her mother said rather sharply that she had had a lot of half-term treats, and it was time to settle before going to school next day.

After some negotiation, they reached an agreement that she could eat her supper and then her father would take her to the neighbour's house for ten minutes. She sat at her father's feet as he asked her about the party, and she was suddenly able to look at Georgie with a different expression, then reaching forward to tickle him fondly. As Monica left the room to get supper, she paused to exchange a brief peacemaking hug with her daughter.

This is a fairly typical family scene. A healthy, developing baby is playing. His play looks like work, in that he is engrossed in trying to reach things, to manipulate them in his hands, to control the movement and sounds of the toys. One can see what might be thought of as the beginnings of a capacity to learn, in the way he repeats actions until he has fully mastered them and then goes on to experiment with a different bit of the toy. He has toys that are appropriate to his age and stage of development, but, much more importantly, he has the interest and playful involvement of his two parents. They do not give him undivided attention, but they remain aware of him and what he is doing throughout. He can attract their attention, sometimes by grizzling, sometimes by smiling and giggling. Their enjoyment of him is palpable, and they actively celebrate his achievements, involving the observer in the celebration, offering the baby a new and different relationship with somebody who is outside the family. This playful interaction and celebration of achievements began in the very earliest days of his life, in the to-and-fro of the feeding relationship, the commentary that accompanied nappy changing, and so forth. The "conversations", as it were, began between mother and infant, between father and infant, among the parent–infant threesome, and then among the family foursome.

When his sister comes home, we see a lively, demanding 6-year-old having to come to terms with sharing the attentions of her parents. Holly has to tolerate the fact that sometimes her brother's needs come first. In this observation, she is able to turn to her father when her mother is preoccupied with the baby, and his warm response enables her to get in touch with her warmer feelings for her brother. She is also able, briefly, to manage her really cross feelings about being left out by directing them to the observer. Here we see Holly's parents managing to have both children in mind, to protect Georgie (and the observer!) from Holly's aggression and to help her manage her passionate feelings of injustice in a different way. Holly's need to be making new connections in a wider social world is facilitated and then reinforced by her parents' interest in the party she has been attending. A pragmatic solution to the issue of the promised visit to the neighbours is negotiated without anyone losing face, and Monica's affectionate gesture to Holly on her way out of the room brings together what might have been a split between the parents, with Holly feeling she had manoeuvred her father into going against her mother.

There is little doubt but that Georgie benefits from being a second baby and that Holly's oedipal feelings are mitigated by the reality of having to share her parents with a baby brother. Of course, it is not always the case that the displaced child is accommodating and forgiving. Some siblings never manage to overcome their resentment of their younger, or, indeed, their older, brother or sister. Some parents do not manage to resist their children's determined splitting, and families sometimes divide along lines of gender, appearance, personality, interests, and so forth, with the parents drifting or being driven further and further apart.

As mentioned earlier, there has been a dramatic increase in the number of "unconventional" family groupings in recent years. If asked to define a family, children still tend to say "mother, father, and baby" even if they themselves have never have experienced life in a nuclear family of that kind. Large numbers of children now live with one parent, with a single-sex couple, with grandparents, in foster care, with adoptive parents, or in complex reconstituted families with step-parents and step-siblings. Each variation on the "normal" family constellation presents a different set of challenges for its members, but all have in common the task of preparing the children for life beyond the family and all are subject to the same internal and external tensions arising from primitive experiences of anxiety, love, hatred, envy, and rivalry. A child in a complicated family set-up has to make sense of his experience and find a way to measure it against what he hears about from friends and what is promoted as normal or desirable in the media. There is a very confusing picture here too, with the traditional nuclear family appearing in TV advertisements, while in soap operas the picture is of constantly shifting relationships.

Family and school

Children come to school with a "family in mind". The family experiences and parental relationships internalized during the early months and years will be the backdrop against which they view the new experience. Relationships with teachers and peers will be informed by the way earlier relationships have been negotiated and the degree to which intense emotional experience has been contained. Observations of children during their first few days and weeks in school provide evidence as to their capacity to manage their own anxiety, their capacity to seek out and make use of containment, and their capacity to relate cooperatively with peers. Each will have a different transference relationship to their teacher depending on what they have internalized from their early experience of being parented. It needs to be stressed that what becomes manifest in the transference between a teacher and pupil cannot be taken as an exact representation of the child's actual parent. If the child seems always to expect a harsh or critical response from a teacher, it may indicate that his parents are exacting. On the other hand, it may be that they are actually soft and forgiving and cannot understand why they have such an anxious child. The internal world is not a replica of the external world; rather, it is a complex combination of experience and what the child has made of it.

Just as children approach school with a family in mind, parents approach school with a "school in mind". Conscious and unconscious memories and feelings about their own experience of formal education are stirred up when their child starts school, and these have an impact on the way they, as parents, are able to interact with schools and teachers. This happens at an individual level, but it also happens at a group level in that multigenerational, extended families tend to have a fairly fixed idea about education. This is, of course, partly driven by historical, sociological, or economic factors, but it is also a question of internal family dynamics.

Returning to Meltzer and Harris's paper about family functioning and styles and "cultural patterns of educability", they identify a number of different family types. Looking at these nearly twenty years later, the list seems incomplete and some of the categories somewhat class- or culture-bound. However, it remains a useful formulation, and I shall give a brief summary.

The first family type is called the *Couple Family* and is characterized as having a parental couple who work together to share the functions of parenting and family life. There is concern for the development, socialization, and education of the children, and there is care for dependent members of the family. The family interacts with the community but is able to operate independently of it, withdrawing into its own private world. This kind of family ranks high in terms of introjective function.

The *Doll's House Family* lives in a kind of perpetual latency, slavishly conformist and conventional. There is respect for authority and institutions (police, doctors, teachers, etc.) but beneath the acceptance of their own inferiority is a real sense of moral superiority. This kind of family does not easily tolerate difference in its midst.

The *Matriarchal Family* is one with an absent or inadequate father, where the mother assumes all the introjective functions. The *Patriarchal Family* is one in which the mother is absent or eclipsed. This family is characterized by a sense of proud independence.

The *Gang-Family* includes a variety of styles, all based on the clinging together of family members around a series of agreed principles. These are not generally based on concern for the children or their developmental needs, although there will be a fierce avowal of the importance of blood connections and a distancing of the family from the wider community. Expressions of love towards children may be somewhat sentimental, indulgent, or seductive, and there is a manic cheerfulness rather than a well-founded optimism about life. This kind of family, according to the authors, seek affirmation of their lifestyle and are tenacious in getting what they consider to be their fair share of society's resources. Gang families are essentially narcissistic and demand total loyalty from their members.

Lastly, the *Reversed Family* lives in a precarious, paranoid state in which introjective functions are absent, or virtually so. Splitting and projection predominate, and there is a tendency towards the illegal in terms of propping up a struggling family economy.

This survey of family styles is useful in that it draws attention to the fact that families, as groups, not only have different ways of managing their internal dynamics but also have different ways of relating to the outside world. Families are more or less narcissistic, more or less adaptable, more or less judgemental about others, and more or less open to new and different influences. All of this will determine the way in which they view formal education and the way in which they manage their children's transition from home to school. The primary task of the family is to introduce the baby to the world in stages and to prepare him for moving out of the family into the wider social context. The first major step for most children is to make the transition from home to nursery or infant school. At this point, the school takes on some of what was exclusively the family's role and continues to share that responsibility for at least the next eleven years, and probably longer.

Meltzer and Harris's formulation of the function of the family could serve as a description of the function of a school. Like the family, the school seeks to promulgate love and hope, to contain pain, and to promote thinking. Like the family, the school has a responsibility for protecting children through their formative years and preparing them for the adult world. It is worth noting that children develop a transference to the school as a whole as well as to different individuals within it. This may be particularly important idea when thinking about children who do not have a secure family base of their own or who seem unable to make use of one-to-one relationships with peers or with particular teachers. Children who find the intimacy of one-to-one relationships too threatening may have much to gain from the school institution (the building, the uniform, the routines, and the rituals) as a container for their anxiety.

Partnership with parents

In the late 1990s and early years of the twenty-first century, there has been an emphasis placed on the idea of "partnership with parents". Successive governments have promised greater parental choice, and parents have been encouraged to take an active part in their children's school life. Primary schools have become open to offers of help from parents, and teachers are expected to make themselves far more available to parents than hitherto. Governing bodies include parent representatives, and there is often a busy social calendar for parents who want to be part of the school community.

It is, however, no simple matter for parents to hand over their child into the care of a teacher. Even the families who have prepared for the event and who have a positive view of education find that the actual hand-over requires a huge leap of faith. It is the first serious test of their capacity to let their child move on and be subject to unknown, non-family influences. It requires that they have confidence in the child's capacity to cope and confidence in the strength of their family culture, the base to which the child will return. It requires that they support the child in returning to school even when he begs to stay at home, as if being sent away is the ultimate cruelty. It also requires that they cope with renewed feelings of rivalry and jealousy when their child falls in love with his teacher and idealizes his friends' families.

The task of letting children go will be much more difficult for families who have not been able to take the first steps towards separation and individuation. It will also be hard for parents who have ambivalent or downright hostile feelings towards education. If their own experiences of school were negative, they may consciously want something better for their children, but the unconscious communication may be that schools are unfriendly or dangerous places. Children arrive at school carrying the burden of their parent's hopes and expectations, both conscious and unconscious. Even at 5 years of age they will be aware of tensions and will feel their loyalties being stretched. How do you engage with school when Mummy does not want you to go and Daddy says the teachers are idiots? Fortunately, this kind of dynamic is relatively rare, especially in the early years of primary school. This may be because many parents whose own education ended in failure still have happy memories of primary school. Secondary education is usually the target of all the bitterness and blame. For some parents, being able to be closely involved in their children's primary school gives them a second chance to experience the energy and excitement of early learning. Primary schools are often diligent in trying to involve parents who are timid about coming into the school, particularly parents who are newcomers to the country and do not share the language and culture of the school. This is vital if children are not to become alienated from their own families, or alienated from school because of family loyalties.

Relationships between parents and schools are fertile ground for splitting and projection. Children may unwittingly contribute to inbuilt unconscious doubts and suspicions in their parents, or they may, as they get older, very deliberately exploit potential splits by misreporting one or other party. Children and adolescents sometimes go home and complain about unfair treatment at school, intent on gaining their parents' sympathy or on causing problems for a hated teacher. Similarly, it is very easy for teachers to get caught up in rivalrous conflict with parents, convincing themselves that they are the ones with the insight and that they understand the child better than the parents. Children will sometimes convince teachers that they are misunderstood at home or that they are deprived or ill-treated. Of course, the ill treatment or neglect is sometimes a reality on which a teacher must act, and schools are alert to this possibility. All of this points to the need for teachers and parents to talk to each other and share their views.

Relationships between parents and schools become much more problematic for both parties when children are in difficulties. The experience of being called in to see the head teacher is one that most parents absolutely dread. When asked about it, parents have said that they felt as if they were back in school themselves, being called to account for some terrible misdemeanour. All sorts of memories flooded in and made it difficult to hold on to their identity as adults and parents. One couple felt that they were going to be told that they were bad parents, that they were to blame for their children's difficulties. A single mother said that she was sure that the head was going to say it was all because her son had no father. Whether the problem is one of poor academic performance or bad behaviour, parents often report that they feel reduced, criticized, and blamed before the interview even begins.

A parent's response to these feelings will depend on their own internal world and their family style. Meltzer and Harris's Doll's House couple might be overly compliant and apologetic, the Gang-Family openly compliant but privately rather contemptuous, and the Reversed Family openly contemptuous and entirely out of touch with any anxiety. The Couple Family—the family that is aware of their feelings, able to think about them—is more likely to be able forge a genuine partnership with the school. Of course, this kind of *reflective function* depends in equal measure on the receptivity of the school institution.

Assessment, evaluation, and inspection

In the early part of the twentieth century, the classroom was a much more private place than it is now. In books and later in films, the classroom was characterized as a place where teacher and pupils battled it out behind a closed door, subject only to the occasional, usually unwelcome, visit from the headmaster. Parents were certainly not expected to "trespass" on school territory, unless invited to attend school ceremonies or summoned into the headmaster's presence to account for their child's shortcomings.

By comparison, the classroom at the beginning of the twenty-first century is a very public place. Gone are many of the high-windowed, brick-built schools; instead, there is an emphasis on glass, on moveable partitions, on open plan and multi-purpose design. Video surveillance cameras range around the school perimeter, and extra staff watch over playgrounds and dinner halls. It is now the norm for there to be more than one adult in the room with the children. There are classroom assistants, support teachers, mentors, parent helpers; there are advisory teachers, inspectors, and practice placement supervisors. Teachers move freely between each other's classrooms, parents come and go. There are peer-evaluation processes, quality-assurance measures, and inspections at every level.

While many of these developments are to be welcomed as steps towards greater transparency, greater accountability, and the eradication of abusive practices, they have served to leave the pupil and the teacher in a very exposed position. If teachers, pupils, or both, are struggling, their struggle is likely to be a very public one. It is also likely to have very public consequences. Schools are judged on their teachers' performance, and their teachers' performance is judged on their pupils' results. In the current climate, SATs results, Ofsted reports, league tables, and exclusion rates are highly significant indices of success or failure. The benefits in terms of the raising of baseline standards in literacy and numeracy are undeniable. However, the costs have perhaps not yet been fully counted. Andrew Cooper (2001) makes a cogent argument for the threat to creativity which is embodied in a culture of regulation and inspection. He suggests that the current enthusiasm for audit is borne out of a fear of institutional failure (mistakes and disasters) and a deep-rooted need to locate blame for such failure outside ourselves. He further suggests that "We have all bought into it, have allowed it to occupy our thinking; at the political level we are deeply implicated in its development by virtue of our activity or passivity as citizens."

The purpose of this chapter is to look, not at the socio-political implications, but at the emotional experience, for individual teachers and pupils, of being subject to assessment, evaluation, and inspection. Educationalists involved in this kind of strategic approach to raising standards would argue that the current procedures are designed to be fair and that children very quickly become familiar and comfortable with the experience of being tested. They further argue that learning to manage pressure and perform under stress is an important lesson and one that must be learned if individuals are to be able to compete in the world of work. The argument rests on an assumption that children will be motivated to succeed and that if they fail, they will be motivated to work harder. This takes little account of the devastating effects of repeated experiences of failure. Just as punishment, of itself, rarely results in reformation, failure, of itself, rarely results in determination to succeed. It more often results in determination to avoid further humiliation by avoiding further assessment.

Of course, assessment has always been part of education. It may be that the very fact that these processes are now so much a part of the fabric means that the experience becomes more manageable. There is no longer quite the same focus on just two or three major days of reckoning. In the 1950s and 1960s, the eleven-plus examination underpinned the system and hovered threateningly on the horizon for all primary school pupils. Everything rested on one day at a desk in a school hall or gym, facing a terrifyingly unfamiliar *printed* examination paper. The results would divide the class in half, usually along a line that the pupils could have predicted as accurately as the staff without anybody having to take the test. Friends vowed that they would not be split apart, but awkwardness crept in over the summer break. In September the two newly defined groups set off in different directions in different uniforms, with a very clear message as to who had a bright future to look forward to and who would have to make do with second-best. Mobility between the two worlds was possible, but only for the most robust and determined. The current situation, with all its flaws, does not replicate that degree of brutality.

Being observed and being assessed

What, then, of the internal situation? How does all of this correlate to what is going on within the individual at the different stages of development? At what stage of development does being observed begin to carry with it notions of being judged or assessed in some way? Infant and young-child observation in family or community settings tells us that, on the whole, very young children are not persecuted by being watched. They want to feel that they can interest adults—most importantly, their primary carers—and that they can show off their skills and achievements. Indeed, it is through being watched attentively that a child has the experience of being thought about. Most children in nursery settings, for example, will actively seek adult attention. If there is a limited amount available, they will compete for it. At this early stage, it is often possible, through observation, to pick out those who fight for attention and those who give up and turn away. Among those who fight will be some who do so with an edge of ruthlessness and no concern for the needs of others. Others will be more aware of peers and better able to share the attention. Of those who turn away, some will find ways of occupying themselves, of managing their anxiety, while others will drift or switch off.

In ordinary good-enough circumstances, what these nursery children are seeking is the kind of affirmation they are used to receiving from their mother or primary caregiver. Many are having to adjust to a new degree of separation from mother and home and are seeking reassurance from other adults, or are failing to do so. For some, the early experiences may have been less positive, and their ruthless demands may be a desperate bid for a compensatory experience. Similarly, lack of protest, where protest might seem appropriate, may be learned "good behaviour" but may, alternatively, be an indicator of depression, of a child having given up hope of being noticed as special or important. These points are laboured here because they link with what we have written about the roots of learning in infancy and early childhood. Learning begins within a relationship: the infant has an experience of a mother who actively thinks about her child's experience in order to understand his anxiety and meet his need. The infant registers the mother's loving gaze, and when the to-and-fro of reciprocity goes well, a lively, playful relationship develops in which the child's achievements are welcomed and celebrated (see chapters 3 and 11). This is often the point at which some infants, for whatever reason, do not internalize a containing experience and are left with a high level of anxiety and internal irritability. This may be the beginnings of an internal structure that will be ill-equipped to withstand the pressure of having to compete and of being judged.

Of course, even the most benign observer can become a persecutor in the mind of the individual or group being observed. Becoming aware of being watched means that the individual becomes aware of what he is doing. If there is discomfort with what he is doing, the likelihood is that this will be projected into the observer, who then becomes an unwelcome presence.

AN ILLUSTRATION FROM AN OBSERVATION OF A 3-YEAR-OLD

Kevin was leaning over into his baby brother's cot, having insisted that he wanted to give the baby a goodnight kiss. He stopped still at a distance of about six inches from Liam's face and stared into his eyes. He looked anything but loving at that moment, and I felt concerned about what he might be going to do next. I noticed that his fingers, which were holding tightly to the rails of the cot, were flexing in a rather menacing way. His grip suddenly slipped so that he almost landed on top of Liam's head. He recovered his balance and seemed suddenly to become aware of my presence. He threw me a hostile glance, covered his face, and ran off into the kitchen, where he buried his face in his mother's lap. I followed, and he peeped out at me from between his fingers. He then lifted his head and stared at me long and hard until I began to feel very uncomfortable. I felt that he had read my mind—or, rather, that he thought I had read his!

Defensive mechanisms at work in the face of assessment

This kind of projective mechanism remains at the root of many of our reactions to the experience of being observed, assessed, or examined. Alex Coren (1997) suggests that in the transference, we make our assessors into whatever we want or need them to be:

> This externalisation of what one could term the super-ego, or conscience, then comes back to haunt us in a similar fashion to other objects that are or have been able to arouse guilt, discomfort or feelings of inadequacy, and are thus capable of predisposing us to a host of potential persecutory anxieties. [p. 162]

We try to rid ourselves of the discomfort of being under scrutiny in a variety of ways, most readily by demonizing the inspectors, the markers, the exam paper itself. If we can dismiss the system as unfair, we go some way towards convincing ourselves that the outcome is unimportant. If we can lay the blame for anticipated failure at somebody else's door (teacher, head teacher, local authority, government) we go some way towards protecting ourselves from feelings of inadequacy, responsibility, or guilt.

What cannot be escaped is the fact that all forms of testing or appraisal carry with them the possibility of success and the fear of failure. They underline the fact that we cannot all be the same. We are divided by our abilities and our achievements, as well as by our environmental circumstances. To do well means that others do less well, or they fail. To succeed brings pleasure and satisfaction but can also bring feelings of discomfort about having triumphed over those who have failed. We may also harbour a growing fear that all we have done is postpone the day when we will be found out, exposed as undeserving or fraudulent. The most common pre-inspection dream (as related by a group of teachers) is of finding oneself in a public place without clothes, facing an audience without one's notes, teaching an unruly group of children without a lesson plan. A colleague once told me that her dream was of being in an airport in a bikini when she knew only too well that she had tickets for a ski trip!

The fear of being ill-equipped and unequal to the task runs very deep and is as real for teachers and parents as it is for the nursery children who are taking their first steps into a world where comparison with others becomes a formalized, external reality. The remainder of this chapter looks in more detail at some of the forms of assessment that are a part of the contemporary system and at some of the effects on individuals, groups, and institutions. The mechanisms by which teachers and pupils are evaluated will go on changing, but the internal dynamics remain the same.

Positive aspects of assessment

There is no doubt that for some children, and for some adults, there are a number of positives in being assessed or evaluated. The framework of examinations—be it end-of-year exams or a timetable of regular submissions—can perform a valuable function in providing a containing structure. It offers a timetable, a timescale to which individuals can work, and a structure to hold the anxiety that might otherwise be much more scattered and uncontained. It may be that a test usefully brings individuals up against what they don't know and what they need to work on. For some, it is an important exercise in reality testing and works against tendencies to deny difficulties or to avoid the experience of "not knowing". Doing well in a test or finding oneself valued for one's work in the case of a peer-evaluation process can be very affirming to the personality.

Standard Attainment Tests (SATs)

The following is an extract from an observation in a Year Two classroom (7-year-olds). It is written by a support teacher and shows something of the impact of this early assessment experience on children, parents, and teacher. It is also revealing in terms of what the observer thinks of the system!

> I come in and immediately realize it's a SATs day. The tables are arranged so that children will not be sitting near each other. Sharp pencils and test papers are laid out ready. I look across the room to Mr G and raise my eyebrows and smile at him, indicating the test papers with my eyes. He grimaces. William comes in with his mother and suddenly clings to her, with his arms fast around her waist. He buries his head in her jumper. Bemused, she disentangles herself gently. He gestures towards the tables. Mr G asks him to come and sit down and discourages the other children from lingering around the tables. One of the mothers notices the test papers and says, "Oh God, it's SATs!" The parents start to pass this news around in loud whispers. Mr G is extremely calm and authoritative as he ushers parents out and children in.
>
> There seem to be a lot of children absent—about a quarter of the class. When the class is assembled on the carpet, Mr G takes the register, making no comment on the number of absences. He then tells the children they are going to have a spelling test. He wants to go through with them some of the things they have learned about spelling. He asks what the trick is when they hear a word and want to try to work out how it is spelled. Tyrone is talking to his neighbour. Mr G asks him to be quiet, but Tyrone carries on talking, and Mr G tells him, exasperatedly, to stand up. He asks him if he will be able to be quiet, because if not,

he will have to leave the room. Tyrone stares back with a set jaw. Mr G says he is not going to wait all day. Tyrone mumbles defiantly "Don't know", and Mr G shouts at him to go and sit at a distant table. Tyrone shuffles over to the table and flops onto a chair. Mr G is flushed and looks tired.

Mr G asks Natalie if she can remember what to do when thinking about a difficult spelling. Natalie answers confidently that you say it to yourself and pull it out of your mouth. She puts her hands in front of her mouth, thumb and forefinger together, and slowly draws them apart in a horizontal line. The group relaxes a little, and several of the children repeat the gesture. Mr G congratulates Natalie and calls Tyrone back, sitting him at his feet and ruffling his hair in a forgiving gesture. One at a time, the children are told where they should sit. Mr G asks me to supervise three tables. The children go to their places. Keith moves his chair to be closer to his neighbour and has to be told to move away again. He looks terrified. Janine lays her head on the table in front of her. The children look very small with their clean, multi-page A4 test papers laid out in front of them.

Standard Attainment Tests were introduced on the heels of the National Curriculum in 1998. They are administered at ages 7, 9, and 11 years and are designed to fulfil a number of assessment purposes. They are indicators of how each individual child is performing, and what potential there may be for future development. They simultaneously provide teachers, senior management teams, governors, and local authorities with a measure of the success or otherwise of the school as a whole. They are, therefore, massively important and become the focus for a great deal of anxiety. The fact that so much depends on the overall results (in terms of league-table position, budget, etc.) creates enormous tension. Schools do sometimes feel driven to find ways to achieve the best possible profile, even if it means doing things that are not necessarily in the best interests of the children. One head teacher admitted that she is always tempted to take opportunities to exclude problematic children in SATs week. She justified this to herself on the grounds that it was both to protect the children from another experience of failure and to bolster the shaky confidence of classroom teachers.

The youngest group of children do not concern themselves with the wider implications of this externally imposed set of tests. They will, however, be all too aware of any manifestations of anxiety in their parents and teachers. They will also be very well aware that it is a competition and that their classmates are also their rivals. For many, the mere fact of being one child in a class of many stirs up powerful feelings of sibling rivalry. The tests then play directly into those unconscious preoccupations with who is the best and who is Mummy's (teacher's) favourite child. Unconscious strategies to deal with these uncomfortable and unwanted feelings will be many and various, and at this early stage of development, probably relatively transparent. Children may become fractious, demanding, giggly, restless, or avoidant. They may equally become withdrawn or tearful. Some wet themselves, soil, or throw-up. Others deny any anxiety and appear to relish the opportunity to show off their talents. A few will, of course, be able to take the experience in their stride, keen to do well but resilient enough to manage disappointment.

League tables

The league table is the very embodiment of the "market-driven" system. Schools at the top jealously guard their position, while schools at the other end of the scale are left to struggle with the demoralizing effects of being publicly identified as "bottom of the class". The new "value-added" system is designed to try to recognize that schools start from different positions in terms of local environment and intake. While schools in deprived areas can show improvement, they can never really compete with their better-endowed neighbours. In the 1970s and 1980s, so many of the reforms that came into place with the comprehensive system were designed to end the socially divisive effects of selective education. The ideal was one in which the individual would measure his progress against his own potential. He would be encouraged to improve his performance but would not be endlessly reminded of his position relative to others.

Streaming was rejected in favour of mixed-ability teaching. Now there is a system in which schools themselves are effectively "streamed". The tables are based on a crude measure of perform-ance, whatever the adjustments that are made to take account of economic and social context. Just as clever individuals or groups of high achievers are able to project their feelings of inadequacy or stupidity into the less able, so the "top" schools are able to locate all the "failure" in their low-achieving neighbours. On an indi-vidual level, failing children become passively despairing or ac-tively destructive. On an institutional level, struggling schools can become places that breed depression or places that unconsciously foster attitudes of envy, resentment, and hostility.

Inspections

Children and young people are very conscious of the importance of Ofsted reports and league tables to their teachers and head teachers. In most schools these days, the desperate need for all to give of their best is made absolutely explicit. For children, the de-mand that they do well for the school's sake has much in common with the demand, spoken or unspoken, that they behave well and are "a credit to their parents". They are then subject to powerful internal forces in the transference, which may be to the benefit of the school or may be absolutely the reverse. Added to this cocktail of individual responses are the effects of group process, and the result is something alarmingly unpredictable.

It is interesting to note just how many teachers report that their classes do wonderfully well in Ofsted week. There is usually a sense of unity, of everybody pulling together to put on the best possible show. This is usually achieved through joining together against a common foe, the team of examiners. The way inspec-tions are set up invites splitting: the school projects all it hatred and fear into the inspectors and is thus able, albeit temporarily, to set aside its own internal differences. If all goes well, this sense of unity and common purpose will probably last throughout the whole process. It may be a very valuable team-building experi-ence that has lasting good effects. On the other hand, if things do not go so well, the internal cracks or splits may begin to show. Government actively fosters a policy of "naming and shaming", and this can all too readily occur within staffrooms and within classrooms. Weak teachers can become the receptacle for every-one's projections: they carry the blame for everybody's failings as well as their own.

Peer evaluation

Being observed, evaluated, or assessed by somebody one knows is a very different experience from that of being inspected by strangers. It is much easier to project hostility and suspicion into a stranger, whom one has no reason to respect and who one will probably never see again—and even easier to project whatever one wants into an anonymous, unseen marker! It all becomes much more difficult when one's assessor is a close colleague or im-mediate line-manager. When there is a real, ongoing relationship between the two parties, the mixture of conscious and unconscious processes becomes much more difficult to disentangle.

Some peer-observation exercises are set up as a support sys-tem rather than as an evaluation process. Even when this works well—as it sometimes does—it is impossible for those involved to be entirely free of feelings of being judged. There may not be any external repercussions, but there are likely to be internal ones. Such encounters can never be entirely free from competitiveness and envy, and the accompanying fear of retaliation or feelings of guilt at having triumphed over a "sibling".

Where peer evaluation carries with it real, external consequenc-es (such as the threshold payments introduced for some teachers in 2002 at the discretion of head teachers), it becomes enormously complicated. We all have well-established transference relation-ships to our colleagues, particularly to those who are in some kind of position of authority or power. We have fantasies as to what the head teacher or equivalent thinks of us, whether they are right, and whether we believe that they will be fair in their judgement. We may feel that our managers do not know us or know too much. Faced with the task of convincing them of our capabilities, we may regret having shared moments of vulnerability in the past. We may be suspicious of the motives of managers and, unconsciously, suspicious of our own. All the unconscious processes described in the opening sections of this chapter come into play. If we succeed, will it be deserved or will it be through some manipulation of reality and achieved at the expense of colleagues? If we do not get the rewards, can we bear it that somebody else does? How do we manage our feelings of hostility towards a colleague who seems to be "the preferred sibling"?

The anxieties can be almost as great on the other side of the fence. As an assessor, can we feel capable of making a fair judgement when we know so much about our colleague, or think that we do? What do we do about our ordinary likes and dislikes? How do we manage our own envy and competitiveness? A colleague once told me that when reading through her comments about a mature student's essay, she found that she had written: "This essay was a pleasure to write." She was embarrassed at finding herself acting out her unconscious envy of this student's abilities. A similar process was in operation when an author found that he was repeatedly misspelling the name of a well-known and much respected colleague, as if he could not quite bear to have to defer to the "older sibling" who had got there first and had already produced work of lasting value. It is remarkable how often students misspell the names of their tutors or of well-known authors in essays, as if they cannot actually bear to look too closely at the achievements of their "parental" figures.

When we look at the complexities of the task of peer evaluation, the question has to be asked as to whether it is ever really an appropriate method to use between pupils or students. Peer counselling is currently in the ascendancy in schools and colleges. The forgoing discussion serves, I hope, as a caution against rushing into such schemes without providing adequate structure, training, and supervision. This is apparent even when thinking of the relatively simple idea of circle time in primary schools, or the development arising from this, known as "circle of friends". In the latter scheme, children are asked to help an isolated or disruptive peer to integrate into the class by providing a small support group. The process begins with an invitation for the class as a whole to talk openly about the child's difficulties. Unless it is managed extremely carefully, it can become a very destructive kind of sanctioned splitting, in which some children are able to occupy the moral high ground while others are identified and defined by their problems.

The impact of repeated failure

There is no doubt but that repeated failure has a destructive effect on the individual personality. Michael Rustin (2001) writes:

> Individuals may be motivated by experiences of failure to de-tach themselves from the experience, to disinvest in a setting which is experienced as humiliating or painful, or to defend themselves by attacking the setting and those in authority within it. [p. 203]

Rustin makes the point that this has devastating effects on the individual and on society at large. The child who turns away from education has, as he puts it, no alternative marketplace in which to develop his talents. I recently heard about William, an adoles-cent boy, whose GCSE subjects had been reduced in number over a two-year period from eight to two (English and Maths). He then stopped attending school altogether and told his mother that he was doing so to punish the school so that he would show up as a total failure on their records and they would slip down the league tables to the bottom, where, in his view, they belonged. Such is the power of projection in the face of a devastating external and internal situation, but the tragedy of this story is that in seeking to punish the school, William put himself in the wilderness as far as his own future was concerned.

Repeated failure also has a destructive effect on institutions. Of-sted inspections have the power to identify "failing schools". These are then put under "special measures", which means that they are given a list of goals to achieve in advance of a re-inspection. They are also "punished" by losing control of their budgets and being restricted in their freedom to make new staff appointments. They live under the threat of being taken over by a special team or by being privatized. It is then difficult to retain good staff or to attract new pupils. Ros Moger (1999) has written about the impact on one school of being held under "special measures". She summarizes some of her arguments:

> The paradox for me is that the process of external inspection, set up to raise standards, may well, in the short term, produce im-provement and higher achievement through a closer focusing on the primary task. It may, however, also provoke defensive

responses which are not conducive to long term professional confidence and growth. In psychodynamic terms, the external threat operates as a steady weight which teachers struggle to bear and which pulls them back into "basic assumption" (Bion, 1961) group activity. "Pulling out the stops" in order to survive is what regular inspection demands of them and they rise to the occasion but that leaves them with little energy or confidence for well-integrated and ongoing development work, which all schools require for truly embedded improvement. If you are a teacher who is doing an impossible job on behalf of society and the inspection process tells you that you are bad at that task, then you carry the full guilt for that failure and in the case of Hollydale School you work even harder to repair the damage.

My unanswered question is, could this learning have come about in a less persecutory climate and would it have been qualitatively different? There is a question about the degree to which such learning under such extreme pressure can be sustained.

Written submissions

The very act of committing one's thoughts to paper is riven with potential unconscious meaning. For small children their early attempts at writing and drawing assume enormous significance, and they expect their parents to be as excited and impressed as they are by this concrete proof of their developing capabilities. They very quickly see that these skills are highly prized in the wider world and that mastery of them provides a passport to all kinds of benefits. They very quickly grasp that there are levels of achievement and that their skills will be judged relative to those of their peers. For many children, this is where the trouble begins. Some master the fine motor skills but cannot get beyond the point of copying the written word. They cannot somehow manage to transpose their own ideas or thoughts onto paper and so spend hours producing beautifully neat work, but very little of it. Some have ideas but simply cannot bear the fact that they cannot write as neatly as their neighbour or that their drawing does not look like the image that they had in their mind and wanted to reproduce on paper. These are the children who may start to avoid the moment when things have to be written or, in extreme cases, may do the work and then destroy it because it does not match up to their expectation or because they feel patronized or lied to by the teacher who is telling them it is good. Praise is of little value if it entirely at odds with the child's internal picture of himself. The most envious child may seek to denigrate other children's work or even to steal or spoil it. Some simply lapse into deeper and deeper despair about ever having anything interesting to say or ever being able to get to the bottom of a page without making a mess.

Vestiges of these emotional experiences remain throughout formal education and beyond. It is always an enormously significant moment when a piece of written work is handed in for assessment. The experience is inevitably one of letting go of a little bit of oneself and exposing it for others to see. Alex Coren (1997) makes the interesting point that dissertations are often completed after about nine months' gestation, and so parallels with giving birth have a certain resonance. I think the analogy can be taken further. There is a common experience that accompanies the moment of completing an essay, dissertation, or any piece of writing that has taken time. There is the task of letting the piece go, of letting it stand or fall by its own merits but there is also the task of mourning the loss of the paper you did not write. When you finish a paper, you have that paper and will not have all the others that you might have written instead. Every time you write one paper, it brings to an end the moment when you might have written a different one, rather in the same way that when you have a baby, you have to let go of the idea of the baby or babies that you had in your mind. In a sense, you mourn the baby you did not have. Many people speak of feeling a tremendous sense of loss when they complete a piece of work, almost akin to postpartum depression.

Examination anxiety

Many of the anxieties identified in this chapter crystallize around the challenge of sitting an examination. Even when the outcome is predictable because of assessed course-work, the "final" paper carries with it ideas of "sudden death"—of dramatic success or failure. Will this be the moment when all will be revealed and I will be exposed as a sham—or as a genius? Coren (1997) suggests that "Examinations can therefore represent both the sum total of our projections, and as objects of transference re-evoke previous experiences of being scrutinized, judged, accepted or rejected" (p. 162). An added element is that exams are often placed in such a way as to mark major points of transition: between one school and the next, between school and college or university, and between full-time education and work. Students taking exams at the end of their school or higher-education careers are in the process of leaving an institution but are also leaving one phase in their lives and moving on to a new one. Students who become crippled by exam anxiety are sometimes desperately holding on to a stage of development, unwilling or unready to move on.

Summary

The education system now involves constant re-visiting and re-working of the issues outlined in this chapter. Teachers undergo repeated appraisal and inspection. They are judged by their own and their pupils' achievements. If they are able to observe and reflect on the feelings that the experiences stir up in them, they will be better able to understand their pupils' anxiety and manage the processes in ways that rely less heavily on splitting and denial.

CHAPTER THIRTEEN

Inclusion, exclusion, and self-exclusion

This final chapter focuses on what is an area of particular interest for me. I am including it because it touches on so many of the themes that have been explored in other parts of the book. Much of what I have to say about inclusion and exclusion comes from my own experience in the 1980s of working as a teacher in an off-site unit for 15- and 16-year-old non-attenders. I also worked for a short time as an education welfare officer and more recently have seen a number of "school-phobics" in my clinical practice. However, it was the adolescent truants in the unit who first stimulated my interest in unconscious processes and showed me the relevance of psychoanalytic thinking to understanding the teaching and learning relationship.

In 1987, off-site provision in London was reorganized and our unit closed down. In 1989, the ILEA (Inner London Education Authority) was itself abolished, the boroughs took over the running of their own education services, and "inclusion" became the policy of the moment. In our post-redundancy gloom, my colleagues and I suggested bitterly that they would have to reinvent off-site units in years to come! In my view, it has happened in much the way we predicted. Since the 1990s, after the full implementation of the

National Curriculum and then the introduction of SATs, league tables, and so forth, there has been a proliferation of initiatives designed to address behaviour problems in schools and to improve attendance figures. Behaviour support plans, home–school liaison workers, parent–school contracts, learning mentors, Connexions, and temporary and part-time Pupil Referral Units (PRUs) are all aimed at reducing the numbers of exclusions and tackling the causes of truancy. Each one of these developments, and perhaps particularly the PRUs, has arisen in response to the needs of children who cannot fit into the "one-size-fits-all" or "inclusion-at-all-costs" kind of school system.

I would argue that there will always be a small pupil population who cannot be accommodated in mainstream schools, but who do not meet the criteria for the small number of remaining special schools. These are children and young people who will either find themselves excluded or will voluntarily exclude themselves.

Truancy

Truancy is a symptom, not a disease or a syndrome in its own right. It is for that reason that I tend to use the word *truant* or *non-attender*, rather than to identify something called school phobia, although some children obviously do have phobic reactions to school. The first task when faced with a child who is out of school is to wonder what lies behind or beyond the symptom of his non-attendance. It is usually the case that there are both external and internal factors at play. External factors I count as being aspects of family life, of the community, and of the school, while internal factors are unconscious processes, aspects of the child's internal world.

I am unconvinced that the reason for any child's exclusion or non-attendance can ever be said to be entirely external. It is always the result of a complex interplay between the child's external experiences and his internal world. External factors may push troubled or disadvantaged children over the edge into provoking exclusion from school or into excluding themselves. Once in an ambivalent relationship to school, at whatever age, children become vulnerable to new areas of risk, particularly if they are at odds with their family too and if they go in search of some other kind of individual or group identity.

External factors

Where there is a clearly identifiable external factor, the problem may be relatively easily remedied, given adequate motivation in the relevant parties and, most importantly, adequate resources. A child who is staying away from school because of specific learning difficulties or fear of a particular aspect of the curriculum, whose parents cannot afford the necessary clothing, or who doesn't want to own up to being bullied or to an inability to swallow school meals, can be supported back into full attendance if the problem is tackled. Children and young people who have been excluded as a result of clashes with teachers face a more difficult route back. In clinical work, therapists are often concerned that their child patients will change but their families will not, putting the child in a very difficult position. This always reminds me forcefully of what happens to so many children when they try to re-enter school after an exclusion or period of non-attendance. The children themselves may be in a different frame of mind, but if the school has done no thinking in the interim, they are likely to prepare for the child they knew and unconsciously act in such a way as to provoke a re-enactment of the earlier difficulty.

There is much to be said about ways in which work with families and with schools can be effective to minimize the incidence of exclusion and to support school attendance in communities where poverty, deprivation, unemployment, dislocation, and poor housing creates fertile ground for rebellion or despair. I would not want, in any way, to devalue the work that goes on as part of many of the initiatives I mentioned at the beginning of this chapter.

Internal factors

The particular focus of this chapter, however, is on the small but significant population whose exclusion or truancy is a symptom of severe and debilitating internal difficulties. My perspective could be described as a developmental one, and I am reminded again of the tasks that are embodied in Money-Kyrle's "facts of life" (see chapter 1). To be able to manage school, the child has to acknowl-edge areas of dependency, to recognize the capacities of others, and to be prepared to learn from them without excessive envy. The child needs to be able to give up possession of the mother, to allow for the creativity of the parental couple, and to learn to live alongside "rival babies".

The third "unpalatable truth"—the fact that time passes and, with it, opportunities—is highly relevant to the challenge of learn-ing and formal education. Procrastination and the ensuing regret is something we are probably all familiar with. It is hard to accept that life is finite. Long-term non-attenders are often caught up in just this way of thinking. They fully intend to go to school tomor-row. This becomes "I'll go on Monday. Better to do a whole week." And then, "I'll start after the holiday. Go back with everyone else." And finally, "I think I need a fresh start. A new school would be best." This is not simply laziness or a denial of anxiety. I think it is part of what is so hard about growing up: realizing that oppor-tunities are there, and then they are gone. Some school-refusers get lost in a kind of suspended animation, wanting to perpetuate an idea that their failure to use today's opportunity will have no consequences.

The pupils we worked with in the unit were adolescents, and they considered themselves too grown-up for school. The reality, however, was that we were constantly required to manage acting out of the most infantile kind. Primitive, uncontained anxiety was very near the surface.

In the early 1980s, there was a notion among educationalists that young people of this kind were disaffected because the cur-riculum did not tap into their particular interests and strengths. They needed to be brought into contact with learning through "hooks" or "carrots" in the form of attractive and "relevant" sub-jects and activities. We tried. We offered all kinds of carrots—

outings, videos, music workshops, motor mechanics, horse riding, skating, and so on. Every new activity would engender excitement and enthusiasm, but the enthusiasm was short-lived. The motivation would be lost in no time, killed off by an inability to wait a week for the next session, disappointment that the new skill did not come immediately, envy of somebody else's skill, loss of confidence, fear of having to travel to the venue, group apathy, and so on. These were adolescents who could not see things through, and this applied as much in ten-pin bowling as it did in GCSE maths.

Finding out about the concepts of projection, transference, and containment, I realized I had a framework for understanding something about why the young people could make so little use of what we were trying to offer. Many of them had felt contained in their primary schools and had done well, only to face the bitter disappointment of being unable to manage secondary transfer. For these pupils, the unit was like going back to a primary school classroom or to a family unit, and they loved it and, of course, hated it. In the transference, they treated us like parents, or aunts and uncles, and each other like siblings, with all that that implies. Rivalry broke out between them, and we were idealized and denigrated by turn. Splitting was extreme. They endlessly tested out our commitment. Just how often would we follow up if they did not attend? Once in the unit, they did their best to provoke us into excluding them, and we often had no choice but to do so. Some could not bear the pain of being offered something that they recognized as being different from what was on offer at home or in their mainstream schools, and they found gestures such as home-made cakes at the end of term absolutely unbearable.

A relatively small number of pupils were able to make use of the "family-sized" institution and took opportunities to catch up on work and rejoin their mainstream schools. Others used the unit as a stepping-stone into some form of employment or further training. What did become clear, however, was that these "successes" were only possible where there had been a positive earlier phase in the child's life. When we were able to give an adolescent an experience that put him back in touch with sustaining objects in his internal world, a good outcome was possible. With others, our best hope was that we had offered something that would lodge somewhere in the individual, such that he might be able to recognize and make use of later opportunities for containment, learning, and development.

Illustrations

The last part of this chapter introduces some of the non-attenders I have known. I hope that these thumbnail sketches will illustrate some of the points made in this chapter and in other parts of this volume.

KENNY

Kenny was typical of a small and possibly shrinking population of truants. His family were "travellers", and they ran a business, a mobile burger bar that they took to race meetings. Kenny's non-attendance was chronic. His family kept him off when they needed him, and if they sent him into school because court action was looming, he would be excluded for challenging the teacher's authority. He did not intend to be rude, but teachers had nothing to offer him. He didn't need to learn anything. Why would he need to go to school? His family would look after him, and the future was set. This view of the world allowed for no change, no difference, no idea of an individual going through an educative process and making some choices. Kenny didn't mind. He was OK so long as nobody questioned him about it or challenged his family's assumptions.

ACACIA ROAD ESTATE

My second illustration runs along a similar theme in that it touches on the power of group pressure, particularly when it has the weight of generations behind it. The "truant" here is a whole estate, a small run-down estate of 1930s blocks on my patch as an education welfare officer. Whenever I set foot on the estate, I would hear whispers—"School Board!" "Truant Catcher!" Doors would slam, bolts be pushed in place, windows closed, lights switched off. I would feel vulnerable, defeated, and filled with indignation. I was being given an experience of what it was like to feel unwanted and impotent—a projection, I think, of the way many of those families felt in relation to schools and other authorities. I now wonder how hard it must have been to live on that estate and want to go to school. The group pressure was, I imagine, almost irresistible. Small children stayed indoors with their parents, and adolescents hung about in gangs.

SHARON

Sharon was 14 years old when she was referred to the clinic because of her refusal to attend school. She was a girl who had done well in primary school, in spite of very poor attendance. Things began to go wrong when she transferred to secondary school. It emerged in my assessment meetings with her that she simply could not find it in herself to do better than the rest of her family. She had a learning-disabled sister, a physically disabled father, and a very depressed mother. She felt she was setting herself up as better than her mother, and she could not see it through. Her mother nagged her to go to school but actually colluded with her in a "We'll sort it out tomorrow" approach to the problem. They both blamed the local authority for not offering a change of school.

VALERIE

Another version of the "I'll do it tomorrow" phenomenon was Valerie. She was a clever girl who should have been doing several GCSEs, followed by A levels. However, she had been stuck since primary school in an angry, resentful impasse. She was not going to go through the drudgery of coursework. Why couldn't they just test her, and then they would see that she could do it if she wanted to? She had made a few TV appearances as a child actress and had ideas about instant fame. She could not face what might have been a real test of her actual abilities and had opted for letting time pass and living on "might-have-beens". She was envious of other people's knowledge and skill but could not learn. In order to learn she would have had to face what she did not know, and this was impossible for her.

MAUREEN

Maureen was clever and talented. She quite suddenly dropped out of school and could not be persuaded to return. Nobody could understand it, and she could not explain. I now think that Maureen was a victim of physical or sexual abuse, and her school-refusal was her way of trying, unconsciously, to tell somebody about it. She did not tell us anything and, as time went on, resorted to acting out her distress in the form of self-harming behaviour. Sitting with her in total silence, I often felt overwhelmed with a sense of powerlessness, as if nothing could be done. It just had to be survived (like abusive treatment). There was also powerful communication of shame and self-loathing. Maureen was eventually admitted to an inpatient unit and received the help she needed. It is worth noting that until these events, Maureen had been no trouble to anyone in school, a quiet compliant girl, getting on with her work at the back of the class.

TRACEY

Tracey was another girl who I now feel sure was involved in an abusive relationship, but her story was rather different. She had been excluded from school for extreme rudeness and only came to the unit under threat of court action. She could not bear to be away from home, and it became clear that she was at the pivotal point in an oedipal triangle. I suspect that there might have been a sexual relationship between her and her handsome, boyish father, but even if that were not the case, there was a collusive relationship between the two of them, shutting out the mother, who was depressed, overweight, and defeated. It seemed that Tracey had to be at home to make sure that the two of them did not get together and exclude her, and perhaps also to make sure that her mother did not come to any actual harm as a result of what was happening, whether in reality or in phantasy.

Mary

Mary had taken on her mother's role in another way. She was caring for her siblings while her mother drank. By the time I met her, she had given up hope of preventing her mother from killing herself with alcohol and was depressed that she and the other children had not been interesting enough to make her mother want to live. Her own future was being sacrificed in favour of her pretty younger sister, and the double tragedy of this story is that the sister, who perhaps had had even less satisfactory early experiences, turned to prostitution at a young age.

Some years later, I heard that Mary was working as a dinner lady at the school she had failed to attend in her adolescent years. She had not married and did not have children, but she was holding down her job and loved the atmosphere in the school kitchens. I have very vivid memories of her presiding over the food at the truancy unit and on outings, enjoying being the one to serve out and adjudicate over "seconds".

Dean

Dean was tied to his mother in a different way. Physically small and underdeveloped for his 15 years, he was, in common parlance, tied to his mother's apron strings. For her, he could do no wrong. He undoubtedly held the balance of power at home, where a mutually adoring twosome kept any potential male partners at bay. At school, he found himself in a very uncomfortable position, a natural target for mockery and bullying and receiving very little support from teachers who found him arrogant and self-righteous. He would whine and his mother flew to his support, whisking him out of school whenever he got into difficulties. At the unit the pattern was repeated, with Dean calling on his mother whenever he got into difficulties.

Stephen

Stephen was another victim of bullying. He had spent the better part of his life in hospital, fighting leukaemia. He was conspicuous—overweight as a side effect of steroids and with thin, baby hair. He was fearful of almost everything except hospital admissions. He had a very positive transference to the hospital, in contrast to the school, which he believed to be full of monstrous cruelty. In the unit, he made an alliance with a boy with badly controlled diabetes and another whose tic caused him to be singled out in a similar way. The three of them seemed to bear testament to how difficult it is to be conspicuous and how powerful is the urge to reject what is seen as different and weak.

DAVID

David was a tall, good-looking boy who had a turbulent relationship with learning and therefore with school and with teachers. He could not bear "not knowing", and so he always knew whatever it was anybody was going to tell him. He came across as arrogant, very full of himself. If we ever found a way through the armour (second skin) and offered him something new, he was deeply suspicious of it, just as he was of the food we offered at lunchtime. He was sure we were telling lies, making it up, just trying to trick him. Here was a boy who was intent on defending himself against any experience of need or dependency. I remember one occasion when he insisted I was mad to suggest that the Thames flowed from west to east through London and then out to sea. Did I think he was stupid? What a mad idea! On another occasion he became hysterical when he thought somebody might have put a tiny piece of cheese on his plate. New knowledge and new food were potentially poisonous.

JONATHAN

Jonathan was a patient in psychotherapy for three years between the ages of 8 and 11. He was refusing to go to school, and he and his mother were caught up in a terrible folie à deux. He was unable to grow up enough to leave her, and she was too dependent on him (unconsciously) to help him to do so. He was an extremely clever boy, but his persecution was such that he could not let his mother out of his sight. His father had died suddenly when he was a baby, and his mother shut herself away in the house with her baby. Jonathan was terrified of everything. Aged 10, he was obsessed with checking locks and switches at home and was constantly worried that the house would catch fire. If anybody came to visit his mother, he stood guard and did not allow her any privacy. She was not allowed to develop a life for herself, and although she said she wanted more space, she did nothing about it. When in therapy, he made a start at a new school, and all went well for a few weeks until his mother began to talk about getting a job. Jonathan hit out at some boys who were teasing him and then kicked the teacher who intervened. He was expelled.

In his therapy, Jonathan could not bear it that I made the decisions about when he came and went, and when I came and went. The fact that I could choose my holiday dates drove him wild. His attacks on me became so violent that I was forced, again and again, to end his session early. Whenever this happened, he was triumphant. Things improved temporarily when the local authority intervened and the parent worker at the clinic offered Jonathan's mother his support (paternal function). Another new school was found. However, the necessary funding was delayed, the start date was put back, and the momentum was lost. Jonathan dug in at home, and his mother requested home tuition.

Casey

My final illustration is Casey, and she holds a very special place in my memory. Casey was lost in a sea of dissatisfaction. There was some real external deprivation in her experience, but it was the internal impoverishment and envy that drove her on. School must have reinforced all her feelings of there never being enough for her. She could not bear to wait for anything. Birthday presents (gold chains to show the world how rich she was) arrived weeks ahead of the date and were described in weight not appearance. Within weeks they would be pawned to fund some new purchase. She was only ever interested in what we were offering—food, outings, refreshments, more food, more outings, and so on. Everything was "boring". It was like trying to fill an empty hole, but we kept on trying to please her, finding ourselves responding over and over again to her projections of neediness and disappointment.

Shortly before she reached school-leaving age, Casey acquired a new puppy, a purer pedigree than anyone else's. The puppy gave way to a fiancée, who was, in turn, rejected in favour of a pregnancy by a boy who, she assured us, would not make any further demands on her and her baby. The baby, she told us, would have everything and would grow up to love her.

A year after she left the unit, I met her in the street with her baby. The baby was expensively dressed, in an elaborate buggy. The sight of the baby clutching a bottle and Casey clutching an ice-cream cone led me to think about what must have been her early experiences and what she had inside herself to draw on now, to meet the needs of her baby. I had a picture of Casey being "topped up" with food by a mother who was unable to give her emotional feeding, just a sort of drip feeding from a bottle. I realized that this was the pattern we had repeated at the unit, giving her tiny tastes of this and that but never addressing the real emptiness.

Food, containment, and learning

I shall finish with a description of meal times at the truancy unit. The links between eating and being able to take in new experiences are very clear, and the behaviour of these non-attenders when food was on offer gave us invaluable insight into their internal worlds, into the reasons why they were not able to make use of the cognitive and emotional nourishment available in school.

The midday meal was delivered from one of the local schools, and some of the young people simply could not wait. They would steal food from the stacked-up tins and urns outside the door. Others would have nothing to do with our food, preferring to spend money in the nearby shops or to shoplift what they fancied. These "self-feeders" were in stark contrast to those who waited patiently as the food was divided up into portions. Some would employ all kinds of tricks and devices to get extra. There was evidence of them feeling they were in competition with lots of other hungry babies, elbowing each other out of the way to make sure they were not left out. Some were phobic about lumpy custard and lumpy gravy. Jelly was a firm favourite with everybody. If the meal was "revolting", they would turn on us and accuse us of starving them or poisoning them. How could we expect them to do lessons if they were hungry or sick? We were often accused of giving ourselves the biggest helpings or of hiding the best bits in the office to eat together later, after they had gone home.

There were some who wanted to eat but could not do so in public. They went away into corners to eat in private. Some could not eat unless they served themselves—again, a refusal to be dependent and a deep suspicion about what poison might be slipped in if they were not watchful. One boy could not stop and would eat until he made himself sick. Some would take lots and leave it, as if reassuring themselves that they need not feel deprived. Sometimes we were accused of cruelty, of making the place too nice, too comfortable, too much food. Sometimes, a well-managed, companionable mealtime was a moment to be treasured, a moment, it seemed, of real containment and potential for development.

Summary

In the unit we had a staff–pupil ratio of about 1:3, a flexible curriculum, and a reasonable budget. It still took all our energy and determination to keep going in the face of what felt like constant crisis management and repeated experiences of disappointment. We gathered every afternoon, like parents talking after the children had gone to bed, trying to puzzle out what had happened during the day. A family-sized group presents staff members with a very particular challenge. I have written elsewhere (chapter 9) about the way the concentrated nature of the transference in a small group can make for extreme emotional responses that are hard to manage. However, in the setting of an off-site unit, it also provided a unique opportunity for productive interlinking of educational and therapeutic aims.

REFERENCES

Alvarez, A. (1989). Developments towards the latency period: Splitting and the need to forget in borderline children. *Journal of Child Psychotherapy, 15* (2).

Bick, E. (1968). The experience of the skin in early object relations. *International Journal of Psychoanalysis, 49*. Reprinted in A. Briggs (Ed.), *Surviving Space* (pp. 55–59). London: Karnac, 2002.

Bick, E. (1986). Further considerations on the function of the skin in early object relations. *British Journal of Psychotherapy, 2* (4). Reprinted in A. Briggs (Ed.), *Surviving Space* (pp. 60–71). London: Karnac, 2002.

Bion, W. R. (1961). *Experiences in Groups.* London: Tavistock Publications.

Bion, W. R. (1962). *Learning from Experience.* London: Heinemann. Reprinted London: Karnac, 1984.

Britton, R. (1989). The missing link: Parental sexuality in the Oedipus complex. In: J. Steiner (Ed.), *The Oedipus Complex Today: Clinical Implications.* London: Karnac.

Britton, R. (1992). The Oedipus situation and the depressive position. In: R. Anderson (Ed.), *Clinical Lectures on Klein and Bion.* London: Routledge.

Canham, H. (2002). Group and gang states of mind. *Journal of Child Psychotherapy, 28* (2): 113–129.

171

Canham, H., & Youell, B. (2000). The developmental and educational context: The emotional experience of learning. In: N. Barwick (Ed.), *Clinical Counselling in Schools*. London: Routledge.

Cooper, A. (2001). The state of mind we're in: Social anxiety, governance and the audit society. *Psychoanalytic Studies, 3* (3/4): 349–362.

Cooper, A., & Lousada, J. (2005). The psychic geography of racism. In: *Borderline Welfare: Feeling and Fear of Feeling in Modern Welfare*. Tavistock Clinic Series. London: Karnac.

Coren, A. (1997). *A Psychodynamic Approach to Education*. London: Sheldon Press.

Dickens, C. (1854). *Hard Times*. London: Penguin Classics, 1995.

Dickinson, E. (1868). Tell all the Truth but tell it slant. In: *The Complete Poems*. London: Faber & Faber, 1970.

Edwards, J. (1999). Kings, queens and factors: The latency period revisited. In: D. Hindle & M. V. Smith (Eds.), *Personality Development: A Psychoanalytic Perspective*. London: Routledge.

Erikson, E. (1950). *Childhood and Society*. London: Penguin.

Freud, S. (1905d). *Three Essays on the Theory of Sexuality. Standard Edition*, 7.

Freud, S. (1909b). Analysis of a phobia in a five-year-old boy. *Standard Edition*, 10.

Freud, S. (1909c). Family romances. *Standard Edition, 9*.

Frosh, S. (1989). Psychoanalysis and racism. In: B. Richards (Ed.), *Crises of the Self: Further Essays on Psychoanalysis and Politics*. London: Free Association Books.

Heaney, S. (1966). *Death of a Naturalist*. London: Faber & Faber.

Jaques, E. (1965). Death and the mid-life crisis. *International Journal of Psychoanalysis. 46*: 502–514.

Klauber, T. (1998). The significance of trauma in work with the parents of severely disturbed children, and its implications with parents in general. *Journal of Child Psychotherapy, 24* (1): 85–107.

Klein, M. (1931). A contribution to the theory of intellectual inhibition. In: *Love, Guilt and Reparation and Other Works 1921–1945*. London: Hogarth Press, 1985.

Lanyado, M., & Horne, A. (Eds.) (1999). *The Handbook of Child Psychotherapy*. London: Routledge

Meltzer, D., & Harris, M. (1986). Family patterns and cultural educability. In: D. Meltzer (Ed.), *Studies in Extended Metapsychology*. Strathtay: Clunie Press.

Miller, L. (2004). Adolescents with learning difficulties: Psychic structures that are not conducive to learning. In: D. Simpson & L. Miller

(Eds.), *Unexpected Gains: Psychotherapy with People with Learning Disabilities.* Tavistock Clinic Series. London: Karnac.

Moger, R. (1999). *What It Is Like to Be a School under Special Measures.* Unpublished MA dissertation.

Money-Kyrle, R. (1968). Cognitive development. *International Journal of Psychoanalysis, 49.* Reprinted in: *The Collected Papers of Roger Money-Kyrle.* Strathtay: Clunie Press, 1978.

Money-Kyrle, R. (1971). The aim of psychoanalysis. *International Journal of Psychoanalysis, 52.* Reprinted in: *The Collected Papers of Roger Money-Kyrle.* Strathtay: Clunie Press, 1978.

Orford, E. (1996). Working with the workers with the troubled child. In: C. Jennings & E. Kennedy (Eds.), *The Reflective Professional in Education.* London: Jessica Kingsley.

Rustin, M. (2001). *Reason and Unreason: Psychoanalysis, Science and Politics.* Middletown, CT: Wesleyan University Press.

Rustin, M., & Rustin, M. (1987). *Narratives of Love and Loss. Studies in Modern Children's Fiction.* London: Verso.

Salzberger-Wittenberg, I. (1970). *Psycho-Analytic Insight and Relationships.* London: Routledge.

Salzberger-Wittenberg, I., Henry, G., & Osborne, E. (1983). *The Emotional Experience of Teaching and Learning.* London: Routledge & Kegan Paul.

Sinason, V. (1986). Secondary mental handicap and its relation to trauma. *Psychoanalytic Psychotherapy, 2:* 131–154.

Steiner, J. (1993). *Psychic Retreats.* London: Routledge.

Syal, M. (1996). *Anita and Me.* London: Flamingo.

Williams, G. (1997). Double deprivation. In: *Internal Landscapes and Foreign Bodies.* London: Karnac. [First published as G. Henry, "Doubly deprived". *Journal of Child Psychotherapy, 3* (1974): 15–28.]

Winnicott, D. W. (1951). Transitional objects and transitional phenomena. In: *Playing and Reality.* London: Routledge, 1971 .

Youell, B. (1999a). From observation to work with a child. *International Journal of Infant Observation, 2* (2).

Youell, B. (1999b). Psychoanalytic psychotherapy with children with EBDs. In: P. Cooper (Ed.), *Understanding and Supporting Children with Emotional and Behavioural Difficulties.* London: Jessica Kingsley.

Youell, B. (2005). Observation in social work practice. In: M. Bower (Ed.), *Psychoanalysis and Social Work Practice.* London: Routledge.

INDEX